PIONEER CHURCHES

Pioneer Churches

Photographs by John de Visser

Text by Harold Kalman

W · W · NORTON & COMPANY · INC ·
NEW YORK

On the title page: the Old Log Church at Whitehorse, Yukon, was built
in 1900 during the Klondike gold rush.

ISBN: 0-393-08754-9

Captions prepared with the assistance of Doug Fetherling.

Design: Peter Moulding

Contents

Foreword

For an architectural historian, the church is perhaps the most fruitful and satisfying subject for study. Houses of worship, more than any other kind of building, stand as superb reminders of the social and cultural values of the pioneers. Religion occupied a vital part of their lives. Some had crossed the ocean for spiritual freedom, others to spread their godly beliefs. Even those whose reasons for coming to North America were more secular still found great security in their religion – one of the few things that they could bring with them intact. They raised their churches with love, devotion, and a great deal of physical effort. Without realizing it, they built a goodly part of themselves into their churches.

American scholars have been quite interested in their church architecture, so I have often had the benefit of their published research. Canadians have been less prolific, making one rely more upon the literature of history than of architecture, and upon such less conventional (but equally rewarding) sources as oral history. Warm thanks are due to the countless ministers, local historians, and other interested people on both sides of the border who kindly answered letters of inquiry, suggested their favourite churches, and volunteered valuable information. Far too many assisted to be mentioned; nevertheless, a number of correspondents deserve to be singled out for their particularly helpful contributions. It is a privilege to thank Earl F. Baumhofer, the Rev. Canon J.D.F. Beattie, Archdeacon H.W. Brandrick, the Rev. Allan Dixon, Zelma Doig, the Rev. M.R. Hinds, Olive Juffs, Gerhardt Kramer, Leonard A. Kuehnert, Edwin McDonald, Olivia Mills, Ken Perry, Clarence J. Peterson, the Rev. T.A. Ramsey, Tom Rumer, Donald T. Tuttle, Charles Vicker, and Ellen D. Wagner. Other persons assisted at closer range. Stan Fillmore opportunely introduced the collaborators, then continued to help as the book progressed. Elisa Anstis, Juliet Pollard, and Mia Killam provided fine assistance with library research. And my particular thanks go to Joan Mackie, who was at once my most constructive critic and my most loving friend.

My greatest debt is an intellectual one owing to the late Professor Donald Drew Egbert. It was under his guidance at Princeton University that I came to appreciate the intimate and intricate relationship that exists between a building and the people who erected it. Professor Egbert was the son of a Congregationalist minister, and the author of the most meaningful essay to have been written on the social and religious meaning of American church architecture. It is with the greatest respect and pleasure that I dedicate this text to his memory.

Harold Kalman
June, 1976

Preface

For a photographer who enjoys the landscape, the church cannot but occupy a warm place in his heart. For a Dutch-born one this is particularly so, because in that flat country the church steeple together with the windmill and the row of poplar trees – "*Canadassen*" as these are called by the Dutch – often provide the only vertical line he can find with which to break the endless horizon.

On this continent the variety of scene is, of course, so much greater that no such single image can be brought to mind. Yet here, too, one can visualize entire regions by simply recalling where the churches are likely to be found: in Newfoundland, often on a high rock and therefore so exposed to the wind that frequently the building is secured with a strong cable or two on the prevailing wind side only; along the eastern seaboard and in the Maritime provinces, frequently the frail-looking clapboard churches seem to seek protection from the Atlantic elements in beautiful stands of trees; in Quebec and New England churches sit like mother hens in the middle of their broods; in the Mennonite area of Ontario the meeting houses appear to be dispersed helter-skelter throughout the countryside, yet, by rotating the Sunday service from one building to the next over the year, no member of the congregation has to ride farther than any other in his horse-drawn carriage.

On the vast western plains the churches are often found all by themselves in the middle of what seems a vast no-man's land, looking as solitary as a single candle on a birthday cake. But, as firmly planted on the soil as they are, here they appear to be more a part of the enormous sky than of the land. In the mountains of the west the opposite is true. Here the churches seem to stretch out of the land to rival the mighty trees.

The practical problems inherent in the production of a book like this are often frustrating. For instance, it must be a sad commentary on the state of our civilization that so many of the churches are either closed permanently or carefully locked, except during services, to guard against theft and vandalism.

Most of the photographs were taken with Leicaflex cameras on Kodachrome film; others with a Hasselblad camera on Ektachrome. To photograph the churches in this book was real joy. The greatest regret, as always in a project like this one, is that some have had to be left out.

John de Visser
June, 1976

Introduction

One of the best ways to understand our pioneer forefathers is through their buildings – the physical embodiment of their needs and aspirations. The buildings that they erected for worship provide the fullest expression of the conscious social and cultural values of their society. This book explores the church architecture of three centuries of pioneers, beginning with the colonists and missionaries who arrived from France, Spain, and England around the year 1600, and ending with those who settled the Plains and the Prairies in the early years of the twentieth century. Neither the date of settlement nor the political boundaries of the time are of interest as much as the fact that the buildings were constructed by recent arrivals in a new land; whether erected in the seventeenth century or the twentieth, the churches were built by pioneers.

The settlers' earliest churches, which were hurriedly assembled as soon as possible after shelter had been provided, were usually built of temporary materials that deteriorated quickly. They were stop-gap buildings built to last but a few years, until the pressures of frontier life eased sufficiently to permit more worthy structures to be erected. These early churches have virtually all disappeared.

This book therefore stresses the first permanent churches erected by the pioneers. The selection emphasizes buildings that are representative of the architecture of their age and society. Because few of the older churches have endured the passing centuries without considerable change, we have often turned to buildings that have been restored, and even to some that have been fully reconstructed.

Two factors shaped the pioneers' churches. First, the inspiration was derived from the buildings of their homeland; second, the raw materials and the primitive technology available to the earliest settlers compelled a simplification of form that comprises the essence of pioneer architecture.

These factors can be seen at work in two Anglican pioneer churches that stand 2,000 miles and two and a half centuries apart. Both churches recall the church architecture of the settlers' English homeland, modified to accommodate the New-World environment. The earlier of the two is the Old Brick Church, built in Isle of Wight County, Virginia, during the first colonization of the American coast in the early years of the seventeenth century. The other is the Church of All Saints at Cannington Manor, in the southeastern corner of Saskatchewan, which dates from the settlement of the Canadian Prairies in the latter years of the nineteenth century.

The Old Brick Church – for the last century it has been known as St. Luke's – was probably built in 1632, making it the oldest Protestant house of worship still standing in America. Its parishioners had recently arrived from England in search of land and opportunity. Some arrived as plantation owners; others were indentured servants contracted to work for five or seven years in return for land of their own. These Virginian settlers, unlike others who sought asylum in North America from persecution in Europe, had no quarrel with the social, political, or religious systems they had left behind. They were loyal to the British crown and devoted to the established Church of England.

Their house of worship reflects the parish churches which they had attended in England. Most of the English prototypes had been built during the medieval period, and hence had features of the Gothic style. Many aspects of the Old Brick Church – from its general shape to its smallest details – recall that style. The tower, roof, windows, and buttresses follow Gothic precedents. The east wall of the church is crowned with a peculiar stepped gable (sometimes known as a "crow-step" gable) that is found in churches of sixteenth-century England, particularly those of the southeastern counties, from which many of the Virginians had come. In the interior, as well, the pioneers followed English medieval precedent by placing the chancel and altar at the end furthest from the tower entrance, and the pulpit along one side of the building.

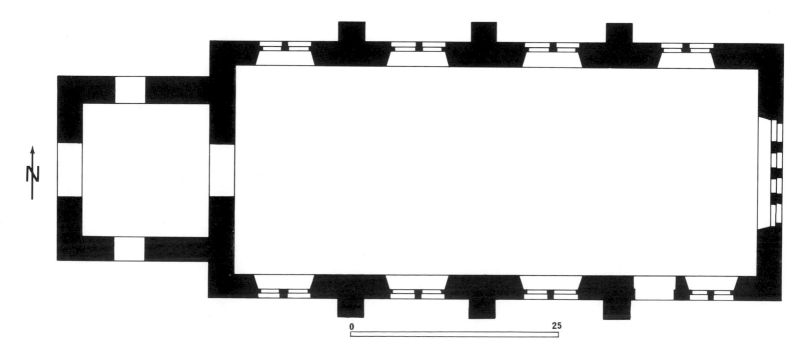

The floor plan of Old Brick Church, Isle of Wight County, Virginia.

At the corners of the tower of the Old Brick Church, bricks are grouped into triple courses in imitation of the stone quoins often used to decorate English buildings. Opposite: The interior of the Old Brick Church.

The Virginia colonists included brickmakers and bricklayers who soon found abundant supplies of clay for their masonry. They also discovered that lime, the necessary ingredient of mortar, could be made from crushed oyster shells, which were readily available.

Half a continent away sits the Church of All Saints at Cannington Manor, Saskatchewan. Built as recently as the 1880s, it is nevertheless a pioneer church. It too derives from the parish churches of the settlers' past, simplified and adapted to suit Prairie technology and unfamiliar building materials.

Cannington Manor was settled by pioneers from England who, like the Virginian settlers of 250 years earlier, could be described as adherents to the established order. The land, located some forty miles from what was then the end of the railroad, was acquired in 1882 by Captain Edward Michell Pierce,

an English gentleman of some refinement who had come to Canada after suffering a bank failure. Pierce advertised in English newspapers for settlers of good breeding and for farm apprentices — mostly public school lads — who would pay one hundred pounds in return for room, board, and a proper education. Their position was similar to that of the indentured servants in Virginia.

In 1883-1885 the settlers built a church and named it after the Gloucestershire family church of Pierce's daughter's husband-to-be. Not only its name was a reminder of the old country; so too was its form. Its body, made cross-shaped by projecting transepts, ends in a prominent bell tower. Like the Old Brick Church, the nave is covered by a gabled roof, the tower by a pyramidal one. The windows again recall Gothic forms, in this case with pointed arches and a hint of tracery.

Across the middle of the tower is a band of woodwork in the form of three-dimensional lozenges that suggest Gothic quatrefoils.

Neither stone nor the ingredients for bricks – the traditional church building materials – were available locally. There was, however, a plentiful supply of timber, so the settlers built their church in wood. They felled the trees, hauled the logs to the site, and on a June day in 1884 all of the townsfolk put up the shell of the building in a "raising bee." Carpenters hewed the logs, chinked the joints, plastered the walls to keep out drafts, and whipsawed the rafters and boards for the roof. The walls were covered with horizontal wood siding to protect the logs from the weather and to disguise the structure's primitive appearance.

The building's bold massing and simple form look some-what naive in contrast to the subtleties of English churches. The combination of entrance tower and steep-roofed nave, however, identifies the structure as an Anglican parish church. By the nineteenth century the Gothic style had long since run its course in England; nevertheless, English church design was dominated by a determined revival of the Gothic manner. Thus the inspiration for All Saints lay in both the surviving Gothic buildings of England and the newer Gothic Revival inter-pretations of them.

In the Old Brick Church and in the Church of All Saints the inspiration from the Old World is realized more through suggestion of particular forms than through direct imitation of them. The precise materials, proportions, and details differ greatly from those of any specific European prototype. The window tracery, the "quoins," the imitation quatrefoils, the ceiling timbers – indeed, almost all of the features – remind a person of a Gothic building without actually *looking* like one.

These two North American pioneer churches can be called *caricatures* of English Gothic churches. They are simplified imitations that exaggerate those aspects that best reveal the source, while eliminating or suppressing less characteristic features. They are "copies" in an associative manner rather than in a literal one. The degree of imitation would have been perfectly adequate to contemporary people even though there was little precise physical resemblance to the source.

Nearly a century ago, a young historian named Frederick Jackson Turner theorized that the primitive conditions of frontier societies led to a constant rebirth of the community's institutions and promoted distinctly American social and political institutions. But harsh frontier conditions do not fully account for the appearance of either the Old Brick Church or the Church of All Saints, neither of which can really be labelled "primitive." On the other hand, architectural historian Harold

The Church of All Saints at Cannington Manor, Saskatchewan, shows evidence of its builders' intention to recreate a traditional English parish church. The window's Gothic arch, and the decoration above the door, suggest the earlier source.

The handsome church of St. Peter and St. Paul at Northleach, Gloucestershire, displays the characteristics of many English parish churches of the Gothic period. English pioneers remembered these features and reproduced many of them in simplified form on their own churches.

Kirker has more recently noted the persistence of the past in frontier architecture. He underlines the cultural conservatism of the immigrants and their dogged determination to reproduce buildings familiar to them from their places of origin. In fact, it is the fusion of these combined forces that produced the characteristics of all pioneer architectural styles: the *change* that the frontier forced upon tradition, and the *continuity* of that tradition.

The church architecture of the North American pioneers displays this singular blend of tradition and modification. Pioneers came to their new homes with an *a priori* notion of what their buildings should look like. The frontier imposed certain physical and sociological conditions that affected the nature of the buildings they erected. It is the interaction between concept and execution in the churches of the pioneers that this book seeks to explore and explain.

OLD BRICK CHURCH, ISLE OF WIGHT COUNTY, VIRGINIA

Known also as St. Luke's, this fine old building (above) with its double-lancet windows and heavy Gothic-like buttresses is the oldest surviving church founded by English pioneers in the United States. The church is believed to have been begun in 1632 to serve the plantations along the James River. Originally, its windows were glazed with clear diamond-shaped pieces of glass. Today's stained glass windows are late-nineteenth-century additions. The parish was an important one in the early days of colonial America, with links to Jacobean England and later – through Colonel Joseph Bridger – to the Council of State for Virginia to Charles II. The church was one of the four places, other than Jamestown, where the General Court of the colony was permitted to convene. As a result, there was some urgency among the parishioners to make the church suitable for this important function, as well as its traditional religious offices.

THE CHURCH OF ALL SAINTS AT CANNINGTON MANOR, SASKATCHEWAN

The Church of All Saints (opposite) is 250 years younger than the Old Brick Church in Virginia, but the simple wooden structure on the Canadian Prairies is also rooted in the traditions of English building. Built in the 1880s by English colonists on land acquired by Captain Edward Michell Pierce, an impecunious English gentleman, the church became the centre of an agricultural community that was named after the Somerset town of Pierce's forbears. The parishioners seem to have preferred breeding racehorses, playing cricket, and staging gala balls to the rigours of agricultural life. Sixteen homes in Cannington Manor boasted pianos. Captain Pierce's daughter later wrote that "it was all such a change from our luxurious life in England, but . . . everything seemed a joke and we were very happy." The little Prairie community failed within a generation.

The French Colonists

One day in June, 1604, a small French fleet under the command of Pierre du Gua, the sieur de Monts, hove to beside a small island in the Bay of Fundy, on the eastern end of the border between the United States and Canada. At Ile Sainte-Croix, as he was later to name the island, he and his crew began to construct their *habitation*, a home for themselves that was also to serve as a base for trading in furs with the Indians. This was the first settlement in what was to become a vast French empire in North America.

The settlement had no chapel; religious services must have been held in a common room. Outside the palisaded compound, the settlers erected a small chapel to minister to the natives; it was built, according to historian Marc Lescarbot, "after the Indian fashion [*batie à la Sauvage*]."

Pierre du Gua's navigator was a career sailor named Samuel de Champlain. In 1615 Champlain became virtual governor of the colony of Quebec on the St. Lawrence River. He brought over the first missionaries from France: four grey-robed Récollet friars, members of the Franciscan order, who were followed by Jesuits, Sulpicians, Ursulines, and others. Most were sent out to convert the native population and — somewhat incidently — to tend to the spiritual needs of the French colonists.

In the same year the newly arrived Récollet fathers erected a chapel at Quebec. It was built in only a month, so it was probably very simply and flimsily constructed. The numerous early mission chapels which followed it seem to have been made of saplings driven into the ground and covered with bark or with clay — perhaps like the one at Ile Sainte-Croix. The only evidence we have of them is a few crude early illustrations.

The European population at Quebec grew slowly. A half-century after the first settlement, the St. Lawrence valley had no more than 2,000 to 3,000 settlers. Acadia (an area now within the boundaries of New Brunswick, Nova Scotia, and Maine) had perhaps one-tenth that amount. Most of the *habitants* lived on long, narrow farms strung along the river between Quebec and Montreal, under a feudal system that was not unlike that of medieval French society. With so few people, there were no formal parishes, although a few communities did erect churches. The settlers — virtually all of whom were Roman

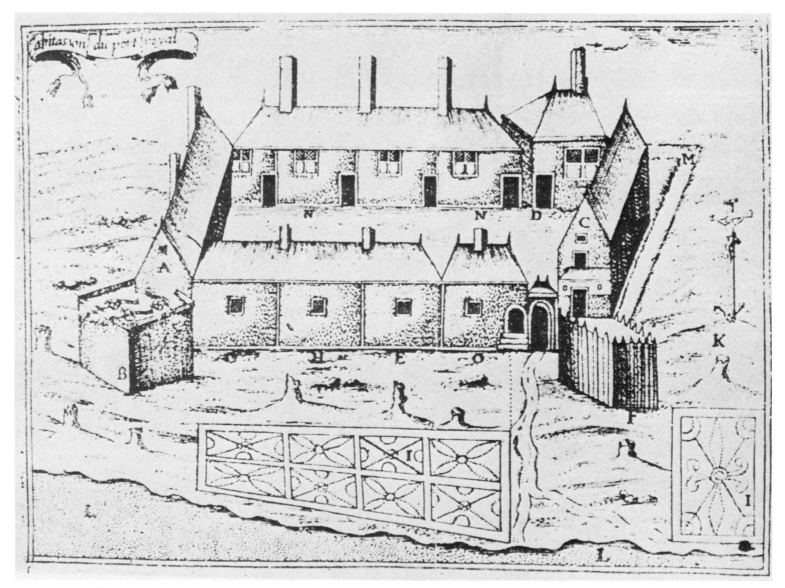

Habitation, Port Royal, Nova Scotia, the first permanent French settlement in America.

Catholics – generally prayed in the mission chapels under the guidance of missionary curés who acted as itinerant priests.

New life was injected into the colony in 1659 with the arrival of the Venerable François Xavier de Laval-Montmorency, who became the first bishop of New France. Born of noble blood and educated from childhood by Jesuits in preparation for the clergy, the thirty-six-year-old Laval was a strict ascetic who reorganized Quebec society from top to bottom. He replaced the authority of the traders with that of the king and the church, and imposed a kind of Catholic puritanism on the colony. Under his vigorous leadership, increased immigration and the high birth rate quadrupled the population in the next thirty years.

Laval launched an active program of church building. He obtained funds from the king, raised money within the communities, and appropriated some of the reserves of the Quebec Seminary, which he had earlier founded and, in part, endowed with his own money. "As it is necessary to build several churches for . . . divine service," instructed Laval, "I order . . . [that funds from the Seminary] shall be spent on the construction of churches."

One of the last churches erected by Laval – and the only one to survive in any condition until our day – is Notre-Dame-des-Victoires, situated in Quebec on the site of Champlain's original settlement. The plot selected was on one side of Place Royale, the old public square that was being rebuilt after a disastrous fire had swept the lower town in the summer of 1682. Notre-Dame was built upon the charred foundations of Champlain's original warehouse. Its cornerstone was laid in 1688.

The church is modest in size, some seventy-two feet long by thirty feet wide. Three tall arched windows admit light along one side and a chapel projects from the other. The present appearance is mainly the result of an 1816 reconstruction. The original façade of Notre-Dame-des-Victoires had a steeper gable, a circular window over an enframed door, and three statue-filled niches in a triangular arrangement. The belfry, called a *clocher*, originally rose over the centre of the church. The walls are built of Beauport stone, some of which was scavenged from the ruins of the old structures on Place Royale.

The original architect of 1688 was Claude Baillif, a native of France who had crossed the Atlantic at the invitation of Bishop Laval. Baillif probably intended a richly decorated façade inspired by the buildings of France. But the church had only a temporary front wall for half a century. The first permanent façade was designed in 1723 by Jean Maillou, a younger man who was a native of Quebec and a friend and associate of Baillif. Maillou developed a simpler *Québecois* manner of building. Architectural historian Luc Noppen explains this change in style: "Instead of the rather confused hypothetical façade of Claude Baillif, Jean Maillou conceived of a simple façade and retained the elements that were at once the most significant and the least difficult to execute: niches and door frames. Actually, it is a case of the adaptation to a local context of a European architecture, academic to boot, whose undertaking had not succeeded in going beyond the project stage, and whose execution had clearly been revealed to be hardly practicable."

In 1759 a large English force led by General James Wolfe beseiged and took Quebec in a battle that signalled the British conquest of New France and the end of the French Empire in North America. Two months of heavy bombardment destroyed much of Quebec; the buildings of Place Royale, including the church, were reduced to burned-out shells of stone. The church

France Bringing the Faith to the Indians, a painting attributed to Frère Luc.

was soon repaired, and has undergone countless alterations inside and out in the subsequent two centuries – most recently in 1967. Nevertheless, much of the masonry that is seen today is original.

The kind of church erected under Bishop Laval and seen at Notre-Dame-des-Victoires became the standard for Quebec parishes in the first half of the eighteenth century. In 1722 Laval's successor as bishop, Jean Baptiste de la Croix Saint-Vallier, officially delimited parishes in New France for the first time. Their borders were, for the most part, the same as those of the old feudal seigniories, but their formal elevation to the rank of parish created a demand for new churches. Many seem to have been based on a scheme that can be seen on one of the few architectural drawings to have survived from that time: a plan and elevation for a parish church signed by Jean Maillou. The Maillou plan shows a three-bay-long church whose length is about twice its width, with a round aspe and a *clocher* over the entrance. The source was the churches of Laval; the application was almost universal.

A lovely church built to the Maillou plan is the parish church of Saint-François-de-Sales, situated at the northeastern tip of the picturesque Ile d'Orléans. A small chapel of wood – the more common material for earlier buildings – had been built at Saint-François in the 1680s; another, twenty years later. Neither church was put together well enough to last, and in 1732 the archdeacon noted that the second was in poor condition. He "ordered the inhabitants and parishioners to collect and bring to the site the stone necessary to build a stone church." Mason Thomas Allard of Quebec was selected as contractor; he simply followed the essentials of the Maillou plan, which by this time had become the standard.

The church's strikingly simple exterior design has a façade with the same plain pyramidal composition as Notre-Dame-des-Victoires, including an arched door and a bull's-eye window inserted beneath the steep roof's "bellcast" eaves (eaves splayed like the flanges of a bell). The proportions are broader

One of the woodcarvings lining the walls of Saint-François-de-Sales.

than those at the earlier Quebec church. The need to widen churches is recorded on an anonymous note written on the back of the Maillou plan: "Church plan by M. Jean Maillou . . . this plan is not wide enough . . . it is only thirty feet [the width of Notre-Dame-des-Victoires and Laval's other parish churches] . . . thirty-six are needed." The nave of Saint-François is indeed thirty-six feet wide.

Saint-François has undergone numerous alterations over the years but none has significantly altered its character. Wood siding was added to the façade in 1864 when it was found that the original wooden statues had rotted badly. A new *clocher* – the church's third – was added at the same time; the roof was covered in tin (common in Quebec) a decade later, after having originally been shingled. The original stone façade was uncovered a few years ago, revealing many similarities to Maillou's Notre-Dame-des-Victoires.

While the outside is austere, the interior has magnificently lavish gilded and painted woodwork. Practically all of the work that is seen today was done in the middle of the nineteenth century, much of it by sculptor André Paquet of Quebec. The walls are panelled in wood, probably all pine. Pairs of Corinthian pilasters (flat strips designed to look like columns) along the nave lead to the richer carving of the walls within the choir. The ornate pulpit, located halfway down the left side of the nave, displays rich carving on every surface and is topped by an imposing canopy. The lavish gilding – done by the nuns in the Quebec hospitals and convents – produces an incomparably rich impression.

A generation ago architectural historian Alan Gowans discovered an original French source for this typical Quebec parish church in Armenonville-les-Gatineaux, about ten miles north of Chartres in the region known as the Ile-de-France. The tiny church of Saint-Pierre-et-Saint-Paul proved to be a rare surviving rural parish church of the seventeenth century that has stood virtually unaltered since its completion in the 1670s – in the age of Laval.

The most striking feature of the Quebec churches is their magnificent interior decoration, lavishly embellished with carved and gilded woodwork. The oldest church interior to survive more or less intact is the lovely chapel of the Ursuline convent in Quebec. Quebec-born sculptor Noël Levasseur was responsible for the fine carved woodwork; he was assisted by his son, François-Noël, and his cousin, Pierre-Noël, part of a dynasty of talented sculptors and artisans that had begun with the arrival from Paris of Noël's grandfather, Jean Levasseur.

At the sacred end of the chapel, behind the altar, rises the Levasseurs' superb *retable* (or "reredos" in English – an ornamental wall). Its composition follows an Italian-French tradition: four Corinthian columns support a rich entablature, and atop the pedimented superstructure the infant Jesus is held by St. Joseph, considered by the Ursulines to be the guardian of New France. Angels with palms sit on either side of him, and Saints Augustine and Ursula stand in the lower niches. Every surface scintillates with reliefs and ornament, and all is covered with painting and gilding. The application of gold leaf was done by the Ursulines themselves.

In the centre of the *retable* hangs a large painting of the Nativity. Before it stands the high altar on which rests the splendid tabernacle for the consecrated bread. The two-tiered

Left: The Processional Chapel, Beaumont, Quebec. Opposite: Ursuline nuns came to Quebec in 1639. Their chapel in Quebec City, begun around 1716, was rebuilt in 1902 using the original components.

tabernacle was carved by Jacques Leblond de Latour in 1709, before the present chapel was begun.

Leblond de Latour, a native of Bordeaux in France, seems to have come to Quebec to teach woodcarving at a school of arts and crafts set up by Bishop Laval at Saint-Joachim – the same school to which architect Claude Baillif likely was attached. With all of this talent at hand, the town of Saint-Joachim developed a fine artistic tradition. Its church continues this heritage in its beautifully decorated interior, finished early in the nineteenth century.

Foremost among the craftsmen who worked there were the father-and-son team François and Thomas Baillarge. Their design for the choir area has made it a stage for the performance of the sacred mass. At the Ursuline convent, the *retable* had been static; at Saint-Joachim, its arrangement into distinct rows of pilasters and columns, separated by dynamic space, brings the entire sanctuary dramatically to life. The conception and execution are wholly within the French tradition – the British conquest did not extinguish the spirit of Quebec Art.

The French presence in North America spread far beyond the St. Lawrence valley. To the east lay Acadia, the land inhabited by the descendants and followers of the original French settlers. In 1755 the Acadians were harshly rounded up by their British conquerors and deported to the American colonies; unwelcome there, many of the exiles ended up as far afield as Louisiana, the West Indies, England, and France. Their goods and livestock were confiscated; their homes destroyed.

Nothing remains of the early Acadian buildings. Their houses were of wood; so too were their churches. Most were unimpressive – one visitor to Port Royal had to be shown the church, "as otherwise I would have taken it for a barn."

Some Acadians began to return to the Maritimes a decade after their expulsion. Most of the extant churches were built some time after the repatriation. The beleaguered Acadians frequently flexed their architectural muscles in a show of nationalism. At Church Point, Nova Scotia, stands the immense church of Sainte-Marie, said to be the largest wooden church in North America. Its 185-foot-high steeple supports three bronze bells weighing almost two tons.

A few thousand dispersed Acadians settled in the Mississippi River valley – where their name became corrupted to

Details of the gilded woodcarving at Saint-Joachim, Quebec. Quebec's tradition of fine church carving had its beginnings in the school of crafts established at Saint-Joachim by Bishop Laval.

"Cajuns"– joining the French inhabitants who had arrived there several generations earlier. The first settlements had been fur-trading forts and Indian missions. From 1699 to 1763 (when the land passed to Spanish ownership), the Mississippi valley was the French colony of Louisiana, and French inhabitants retained their traditions long after that. The colony's capital, New Orleans, lost almost every building from the French pioneer era in a fire in 1788, including the fine church dedicated to St. Louis.

Many of their earliest church buildings in the Mississippi valley had "palisaded" walls made of posts set upright in the ground, rather like the first mission chapels in Quebec. The church erected by Jesuit missionaries at Vincennes, Indiana, shortly after 1702, was built in this manner.

The Vincennes chapel was demolished later in the eighteenth century, but another church built by the French survives at Cahokia, Illinois, today a suburb of St. Louis situated on a narrow channel of the Mississippi. The Church of the Holy Family at Cahokia was built by a method known as *poteaux-sur-sole* ["posts on sill"]. In this technique, massive timber sills, laid directly on levelled ground, support heavy, hewn timber posts about ten to twelve inches wide and about nine inches apart.

Diagonal braces at the corners support the structure. The spaces between the posts are filled with a mixture of rubble stone and lime – a method called *pierrotage* (*pierre* being the French word for "stone"). Channels cut into the posts help hold the filling in place.

In many respects the church looks back to the Quebec buildings of over a century earlier. *Poteaux-sur-sole* construction had been used to some extent in seventeenth-century Quebec, but came to be replaced by stone. In addition, the Cahokian building has many design features in common with a church such as Notre-Dame-des-Victoires: similar dimensions, steep vertical roof (with bellcast eaves at Cahokia), the *clocher* atop the gable, the round-headed doorway, the sculpture niche, and the circular window.

Missionaries from Quebec also struck out toward the Great Lakes. The finest seventeenth-century mission was the one built by the Jesuits for the Huron Indians beside the River Wye, near Georgian Bay on the present-day site of Midland, Ontario. Around 1640 the "Black Robes" built a large mission compound called Sainte-Marie-aux-Hurons. The Hurons were attacked by their Iroquois enemies in 1649, and five of the Jesuit fathers, including the famous St. Jean de Brébeuf, were tortured to death. Sainte-Marie-aux-Hurons was burned to the ground by the Hurons to prevent the Iroquois from occupying it. The mission was reconstructed in 1964.

Chapels at the mission were erected by the Jesuits for both the Indian and the European communities. Both were built in the *poteaux-sur-sole* technique, but here the infill between the posts is composed of two parallel rows of horizontal planks packed with an insulating layer of stone and clay, rather than the stone and lime used at Cahokia. Carpenter Charles Boivin, recently arrived from Rouen, probably designed the mission buildings. This kind of construction using horizontal boards between posts (although not necessarily with the stone insulation) became the standard method in the French hinterland. Survivals of this method occurred as late as the mid-nineteenth century and as far away as the Pacific coast.

The fur traders ventured further westward and were followed by priests and by settlers. Early in the nineteenth century communities of French and of Métis – the French-speaking, Roman Catholic children of French fathers and Indian mothers – began to settle in the valley of the Red River, in the southeastern part of Manitoba. They were administered to by priests and missionaries from the east. One of their few surviving earlier houses of worship is the chapel of Notre-Dame-de-Bonsecours at St. Norbert, Manitoba. This small chapel has been much altered since its erection in the 1870s, yet it still contains a fine and unusual painted ceiling.

The French were eventually out-manoeuvred in North America by the Spanish and the British. The Spanish, in particular, settled in vastly different environmental regions than did the French. Because of this, and in spite of the fact that their religion was the same as that of the French, the Spanish architectural contribution to the frontier was unique.

Saint-François-de-Sales, Ile d'Orléans, Quebec (opposite, above, and below), is typical of the parish churches built from Montreal to the Saguenay River during the eighteenth century. It is a wonder that the handsome wall panellings (added in the nineteenth century, although continuing in the earlier tradition) have survived, since the parish cannot afford to heat the church during the winter.

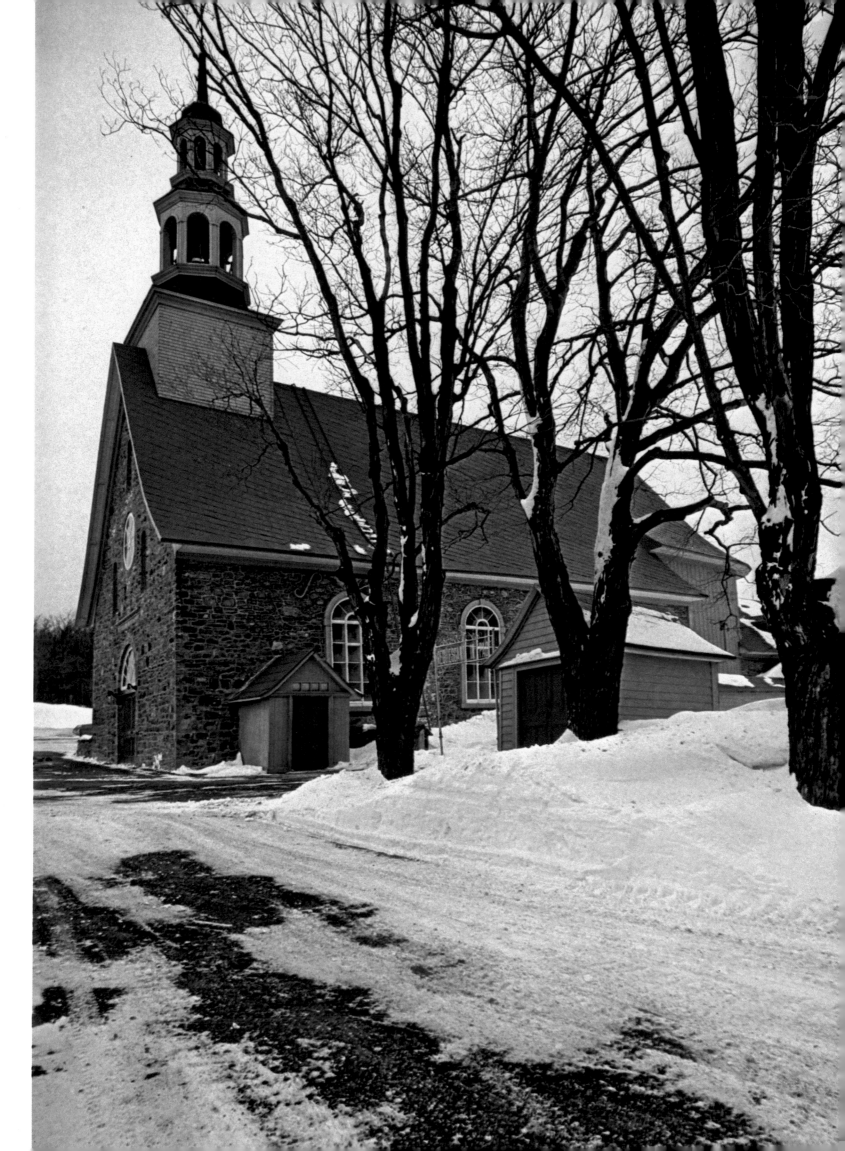

FRANCE IN THE NEW WORLD

The French began colonization of Canada early in the seventeenth century. Many of the first French settlements in what came to be known as New France were established by missionaries. Few of the early churches that they built still survive.

The Ile d'Orléans, only a few miles downriver from Quebec City, was long cut off from the mainstream of Canadian life before construction of a bridge to the mainland in the 1930s. Many fine older buildings are preserved on the island, making this picturesque part of New France a delight to visit.

The lovely church built in 1734 at Saint-François on the Ile d'Orléans (pages 22-23) has a simple exterior, but the interior is embellished with lavishly painted and gilded woodcarving that provides a feast to the eyes. The wall panelling was added in the nineteenth century, although the florid carving between the frames continues the earlier Quebec tradition.

By the eighteenth century, stone had become the most commonly used material for Quebec churches. The colony along the St. Lawrence valley was a century old, and its inhabitants were sufficiently settled to be able to think more about building with permanence. Every farmer found stone strewn all over his fields and had to clear it away before he could plow the land. Stone came to be used for churches, for houses, and even for the fences between the farms. Rubble stone taken off the fields

was bedded deeply in mortar made of sand and lime. Cut stone was usually used only around doors and windows and at the corners. Some buildings had walls as much as four feet thick, enough to keep the people inside cool in summer and warm in winter.

The small church at Cap-de-la-Madeleine (opposite), begun in 1714, is one of the oldest churches still standing in Quebec. It was constructed using this fieldstone technique. A large pilgrimage church was built directly behind it in 1888. The old house of worship was attached to the new one and became a chapel. It has been altered over the years, but still retains its original lines.

In addition to New France, the French claimed the Mississippi valley in 1699. Around 1702 a group of Jesuit missionaries built an Indian chapel at Vincennes, now a town on the Wabash River in the state of Indiana. The missionaries named Vincennes after the Paris suburb best remembered for the mental institution where the Marquis de Sade was detained.

The sketch above is a hypothetical restoration of the Vincennes chapel, based on early descriptions and taken from *Architecture of the Old Northwest Territory* by Rexford Newcomb. It was built by the French in the manner called *poteaux-en-terre* ["posts in the ground"], a method of construction almost certainly inspired by longhouses and other Indian structures. The practice of placing a fire in the middle of the floor and allowing the smoke to escape through a hole in the thatched roof was also learned from the natives. The original worshippers entered the windowless structure through a rough door to pray in candle-lit gloom.

Opposite: The old church at Cap-de-la-Madeleine was begun in 1714. The building survives as a chapel attached to a larger pilgrimage church. Above: the Indian chapel at Vincennes, Indiana.

NOTRE-DAME-DES-VICTOIRES, QUEBEC CITY

The church of Notre-Dame-des-Victoires (opposite), commissioned by Bishop Laval in 1688 – and the only one of Laval's churches to survive – was begun under French architect Claude Baillif and completed by *Québecois* Jean Maillou. Early in the eighteenth century Maillou prepared a plan for a church (above) similar to Notre-Dame-des-Victoires that became the standard for parish churches throughout the colony.

The name of Notre-Dame was changed twice – both times because of miracles that saved the people of New France from British invaders. The church was originally dedicated to the Infant Jesus. In 1690 William Phips led an English naval force against Quebec. Under siege for five days, the citizens were desperate. The annals of the Hôtel-Dieu Hospital reported that:

> As the situation grew more alarming, public prayers redoubled in the city. The citizens had implored the Blessed Virgin to act as their patron saint and protect them. The ladies had pledged word to go on pilgrimage

to the Lower Town church if the Blessed Virgin obtained their liberation.

The ladies were fortuitously heeded. Admiral Phips gave up the siege, and the town was saved. "We did not know how to express our gratitude to the divine Majesty," wrote Mother Anne Bourdon in the annals of the Ursulines, "acknowledging that we had been saved by a stroke of her power as we had not been a party to his victory." Bishop Laval expressed the gratitude of all by decreeing that their church should be renamed Notre-Dame-de-la-Victoire – "Our Lady of Victory."

The second miraculous resistance occurred twenty-one years later, when a second British fleet sailed up the St. Lawrence. They were aided in the attack by land forces approaching from the south. Once more the citizens appealed to the Virgin Mary to save them and once more their prayers were answered. A storm broke out in the Gulf of St. Lawrence, destroying ten warships. The naval attack was abandoned and the army retreated. Afterward the church was renamed Notre-Dame-des-Victoires, signifying the double miracle.

NOTRE-DAME-DE-L'ASSOMPTION, ARICHAT, NOVA SCOTIA

This handsome twin-towered wooden church of Notre-Dame-de-l'Assomption stands at Arichat, a town on a small island off the Cape Breton coast of Nova Scotia. Settlement of Arichat began soon after 1760. The settlers were returning Acadians, descendants and followers of Champlain's original French settlers at Port Royal.

In 1713, at the Treaty of Utrecht, France had ceded Port Royal and all the rest of Nova Scotia's mainland to England, but the French-speaking settlers remained in their homes, stead-fastly refusing to deny their identity. In 1755, on the eve of the Seven Years' War, Governor Charles Lawrence of Nova Scotia lost patience with his French subjects and expelled them from the province. "It is Preremptorily his Majesty's orders," read the proclamation, "that the whole French inhabitants of these Districts be removed."

When the war was over, some of the expelled Acadians returned to Arichat and other towns, and began to rebuild their communities. The church of Notre-Dame-de-l'Assomption, which replaced an earlier chapel, was built mostly in 1837. The church was enlarged when Arichat temporarily became the centre of an episcopal see.

SAINTE-MARIE-AUX-HURONS, MIDLAND, ONTARIO

The founders of Sainte-Marie-among-the-Hurons, Jesuit missionaries Jean de Brébeuf and Jerome Lalemant, were burned to death with three companions by the Iroquois in 1649. Nearly twenty-five years earlier they had transported their proselytizing zeal to the western frontier of what is now vacationland Ontario and northern Michigan. In bringing their mission to the Hurons of this region, they made deadly enemies of the Huron Nations's foes, the Iroquois. Francis Parkman in *The Jesuits in North America in the Seventeenth Century* (1867) tells how Jean de Brébeuf came to carry the Word to this unprepossessing land of forests and lakes.

> Once, when he was among the Neutral Nation, in the winter of 1640, he beheld the ominous apparition of a great cross slowly approaching from the quarter where lay the country of the Iroquois. He told the vision to his comrades.
>
> "What was it like? How large was it?" they eagerly demanded.
>
> "Large enough," replied the priest, "to crucify us all." To explain such phenomena is the province of psychology, and not of history.

The letters of the missionary fathers report what it was like to bring the Gospel to the wilderness. Brébeuf reported in *Relation of What Occurred among the Hurons in the Year 1635:*

> Seeing them, therefore, thus gathered together at the beginning of this year, we resolved to preach publicly to all, and to acquaint them with the reason of our coming into their Country, which is not for their furs, but to declare to them the true God and his son, Jesus Christ, the universal Saviour of our souls. . . . If you ask them who made the sky and its inhabitants, they have no other reply than that they know nothing about it. And when we preach to them of one God, Creator of Heaven and Earth, and of all things, and even when we talk to them of Hell and Paradise and of our other mysteries, the headstrong reply that this is good for our Country and not for theirs; that every Country has its own fashions. But having pointed out to them, by means of a little globe that we had brought, that there is only one world, they remain without reply.

Brébeuf is credited with composing the first Canadian Christmas carol. Originally written in the Huron tongue, it has now been translated into French and English. In English, it runs in part like this:

> 'Twas in the moon of wintertime
> When all the birds had fled,
> That Mighty Gitchi Manitou
> Sent angel choirs instead . . .

Father Jérôme Lalemant, one of Brébeuf's companions in martyrdom, described the mission field in the early seventeenth century. He wrote: "The Ocean which separates us from France sees on its eastern side, only rejoicing, splendour, and bonfires; but on its western, nothing but war, slaughter, and conflagration." About the Iroquois he was equally doleful. "They come like foxes through the woods. They attack like lions. They take flight like birds, disappearing before they have really appeared."

Right: the altar at Sainte-Marie-aux-Hurons, Midland, Ontario.

SAINTE-FAMILLE, ILE D'ORLÉANS, QUEBEC

The church at Sainte-Famille, the first parish to be founded on the Ile d'Orléans, was built by a community that was larger, more affluent, and more ambitious than many in New France. A census taken in 1683 showed that Sainte-Famille was the third largest parish in New France.

The first church at Sainte-Famille, begun in 1669, was one of the earliest stone churches in Quebec. Apparently the builders were not very familiar with their material, because structural problems led to the need for a replacement. Work began in 1743 on an impressive new church (opposite) with two matched towers rather than the customary single *clocher*; and a century later a third spire was added between them. The tall walls are built in the familiar rubble stone technique. The larger-than-life-size statues of the holy family that grace the niches are here temporarily removed for restoration.

The interior (left) contains work by many of Quebec's best craftsmen. The high altar was made in 1749 by the Levasseur family; the wood panelling of the choir was added in the 1820s by the celebrated Thomas Baillargé. The panelling along the nave was added in 1910.

Below is an architectural drawing of the plan of Sainte-Famille.

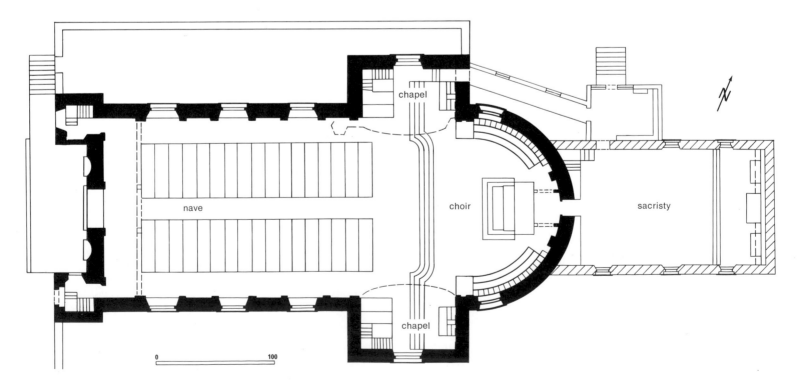

THE CHAPEL AT NEUVILLE, QUEBEC

In addition to its many parish churches, its houses of the religious orders, and its mission chapels for the natives, New France possessed countless smaller chapels and devotional shrines used for private prayer. Many were only occasionally administered to by intinerant priests or missionaries, for in the early days there were far fewer priests than were required. Records show that in some remote places an annual visit by a priest was all that could be managed.

An attractive chapel dating from the first half of the eighteenth century is at Neuville, some twenty miles up the St. Lawrence River from Quebec. It is a processional chapel built as a stage in a road to Calvary, and is dedicated to one of the stations of the cross. The fieldstone chapel (opposite and above) is a parish church in miniature; it is a gem of a building, set in a picturesque landscape.

At the beginning of the eighteenth century, a Jesuit missionary had written to France proclaiming that:

> There remains unknown to Europeans, up to the present time, an immense portion of Canada, beyond the Mississippi River, situated beneath a milder sky, well-inhabited, and abounding in animal and vegetable life. So it is, likewise, with another region far dissimilar to that, around the frozen Hudson Bay . . . lying at the north, plunged in snows and frosts, it even more justly implores aid, as it is afflicted by more weighty ills. Here the society, a few years ago, first began to plant its footsteps.

Not long after the chapel at Neuville was built, Jesuit hopes for expanding the French presence in North America were dashed when the British defeated the French at Quebec City.

SAINT-JOACHIM, QUEBEC

Under Bishop Laval, a fine tradition of woodcarving was developed at a school of arts and crafts at Saint-Joachim-de-Montmorency. Teachers were brought over to the school from France to train native-born artists. The church in that village (above and opposite) is a fine example of this tradition of craftsmanship.

Saint-Joachim lost its first church in the English bombardment of 1759. The present house of worship was consecrated twenty years later, and its fine interior was finished early in the nineteenth century.

THE CHAPEL OF NOTRE-DAME-DE-BONSECOURS, ST. NORBERT, MANITOBA

At the signing in 1794 of Jay's Treaty, the German-born American fur trader John Jacob Astor remarked, "Now the fur trade will build me a fortune." Astor was not alone. There was not a trail through the bush that didn't boast a hidden business magnate disguised in the homespun trousers and leather coat of a *coureur de bois*. These Sindbads of the wilderness, as Washington Irving called them, kept moving westward as the competition for furs grew keener. The fur traders were followed at a safe distance by both priests and settlers.

In 1821 Sir George Simpson wrote to the governors of the Hudson's Bay Company: ". . . It has occurred to me however that Philanthropy is not the exclusive object of our visits to these Northern Regions, but that to it are coupled interested motives, and the Beaver is the grand bone of contention."

The Chapel of Notre-Dame-de-Bonsecours (above), at St. Norbert, Manitoba, is a small reminder of the hurly-burly of the days when the fur trade moved west. It has been much altered since its erection in the 1870s, yet it retains an elaborate and well-preserved painted ceiling (opposite). Its open front exposes the chapel to the elements all year round.

Roadside chapels such as this one came to be common along the routes that the pioneers travelled as they moved westward. On the Canadian Prairies, however, the French Catholic presence was soon overwhelmed by pioneers of many other ethnic and religious backgrounds. The French left behind them a legacy in the form of the Métis people, children of French men and Indian women. Around the time when this chapel was built, the tensions between the Métis and the government in Ottawa was so great that it erupted into violence. In 1869, at the beginning of what came to be known as the Riel Rebellion (named after the Métis leader), the Métis had barricaded the main road near the site of this chapel to force the guarantee of their land rights in the region.

SAINTE-FAMILLE, CAHOKIA, ILLINOIS

Settlement at Cahokia was begun in the spring of 1699 by four priests who, with a small party, paddled by canoe from Quebec to establish a new mission. They chose a spot near the junction of the Mississippi and Missouri rivers. After a number of years, Cahokia acquired a fort and a small community of farmers whose fields were divided into narrow strips like the farms of the St. Lawrence valley. The town never prospered. When the Treaty of Paris was negotiated in 1763 Father Forget du Verger sold the mission property "for a song rather than leave it to the English." During the American Revolutionary War the Cahokians declared themselves to be American sympathizers, but suffered at the hands of both warring factions.

It took the dedicated labours of Father Paul de Saint-Pierre, who came to Cahokia from Baltimore in 1786, to revive the moribund community. One of his most successful endeavours was the construction of the Church of the Holy Family (opposite, above, and right). It was built out of the remains of the house of Father du Verger, which "had been entirely ruined by the English and American troups who have lodged there." Although Father de Saint-Pierre's church is not large, it took thirteen years to erect it because of the town's impoverished state. Its "post-on-sill" construction derives from the methods that had been used in Quebec a century earlier.

SAN ESTEVAN DEL REY, ACOMA, NEW MEXICO

Father Juan Ramírez, the founder of San Estevan (right and below), had no training as an architect, yet he designed a massive and beautiful church that is perfectly suited to the surrounding barren landscape. The enormous twin bell towers seem to guard the building from attack, as does the very location of the church, high atop a lonely mesa.

Much of the labour involved in the monumental task of construction was done by women, girls, and boys. Pueblo men considered this labour beneath them. Apart from fighting wars and hunting game, the men were masters of many crafts, such as spinning, weaving, and carpentry. While they concerned themselves with the church's woodwork, the construction of the adobe brick walls was left to the women.

The immense timbers for the roof beams [*vigas*] apparently were hauled from the San Mateo mountains, some thirty miles from the construction site. Tradition suggests that men carried the timbers on their shoulders, but it is more probable that they were dragged across the desert with the help of oxen. All of the materials – the adobe bricks, the stones, and the *vigas* – had to be hauled up rocky trails to the top of the mesa. The bricks, which each weighed from fifty to sixty pounds, were raised higher and higher as the walls rose, and were finally topped by the *vigas*.

THE CHURCH AND CONVENTO OF SAN JOSÉ, LAGUNA, NEW MEXICO

Franciscan missionaries were the first pioneers of New Mexico. They did much more than bring religion to the natives; they taught them European agriculture and crafts and made them into citizens modelled on those of the civilization they knew at home. The padres designed the mission churches as best they could, with features remembered from Spanish and Mexican architecture. The execution was left to natives, who were accustomed to their own methods of pueblo construction.

San José at Laguna, New Mexico (above and opposite), reflects this blending of traditions. The layout (right) is Spanish; the church is surrounded by a walled forecourt, or *atrio*, and set next to a *convento* with a central *cortile*. But the barren white plastered walls and the cubic forms are Indian. Inside, too, the walls combine Christian and pagan symbols in a riot of brightly coloured design.

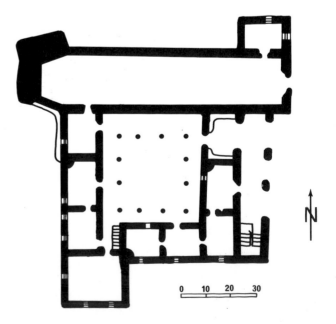

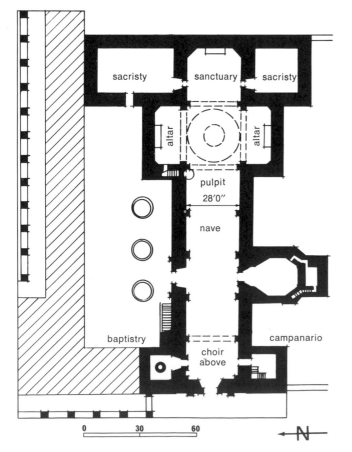

THE MISSIONS OF OLD CALIFORNIA

Mission San Diego de Alcalá (opposite) was the first, and architecturally one of the most attractive, of the California missions. Here the naivete of the New Mexico missions is replaced by a more sophisticated building. The present church, the mission's fifth, was begun in 1808 and completed five years later. Its design is overwhelmingly Spanish because in California the native architectural tradition was weaker than that in New Mexico; the Indians on the west coast generally did not live in permanent settlements.

San Luís Rey de Francia, built in 1811-1815 (above, with a plan to the left), was the most prosperous of the California missions. Almost three thousand Indians resided there at its peak, most of them living in straw-thatched huts in a village two hundred yards from the mission. The Indians tended fertile gardens and orchards outside the compound. Fifty thousand head of cattle grazed in the nearby fields.

SAN JUAN CAPISTRANO, CALIFORNIA

In 1776 Father Junípero Serra, the acclaimed Franciscan priest
who founded the California missions, built a small adobe
chapel (above) dedicated to San Juan Capistrano. A generation
later a domed church (right and opposite) was raised
beside the chapel. Just six years following its construction an
earthquake brought the tower and domes of the church down.
Forty worshippers observing the feast of the Immaculate
Conception were killed, but thirteen hundred other Indians
living at the mission escaped the tragedy. Although the natives
continued to be served, the great church was never restored.

San Juan Capistrano survives today as a ruin; the original
chapel built by Father Serra is a part of it. The chapel is the
only church building left in California in which the great
Franciscan celebrated mass.

The mission is also known as the home of thousands of
swallows who arrive every year on March 19, St. Joseph's Day.
They spend the summer in mud nests in the ruins of the church,
and depart for their winter migration on October 23, St. John's
Day. This unexplained occurrence is marked by yearly fiestas.

Right and opposite: the ruins of the original mission of San Juan
Capistrano, where the swallows nest every summer. It was the greatest
of the California missions.

The Spanish Missionaries

A century before the French had come to the New World in search of precious furs, Spain was sending adventurers to far-away America in pursuit of yet a greater treasure – gold. Spain came to America under no less an authority than that of the Pope. Two papal bulls issued by Alexander VI in 1493 and 1494 gave Spain control over all undiscovered lands west of the Cape Verde Islands. The Spanish *conquistadores* – minor noblemen who lusted for adventure – first gained control of the Caribbean islands, then turned their attention to the South and North American mainland.

Juan Ponce de León was the first to reach the North American mainland. He landed near St. Augustine in 1513 and claimed the area he called "Florida" for the King of Spain. After his death (caused by wounds inflicted by Indians defending their homes) he was followed by Lucas Vásquez de Ayllón. Charles V's instructions to Ayllón in 1523 made it clear that conquest was to be accompanied by conversion:

> Our principal intent in the discovery of new lands is that the inhabitants and natives thereof who are without the light of the knowledge of faith may be brought to understand the truths of our holy Catholic faith, and that they may come to the knowledge thereof and become Christians and be saved, and this is the chief motive you are to bear and hold in this affair, and to this end it is proper that religious persons should accompany you.

The Spanish colonization of Florida and the American southeast never amounted to much. One impressive fortress remains – the Castillo de San Marcos at St. Augustine. The only Spanish church to survive in Florida is the Catholic cathedral in the same city, built at the end of the eighteenth century.

The first significant expedition into the American southwest was led by Juan de Oñate, a wealthy Mexican mine owner who continued the vain search for gold. Oñate was also assigned to establish a colony to protect the northern approaches to Mexico from invasion by the English or the French. He set out in 1598 with soldiers, farmers, slaves, and their families, their baggage crammed into eighty-three wagons and carts. With them came a herd of about 7,000 cattle and eight Franciscan friars. Oñate found no gold but as a result of his expedition the Spanish province of New Mexico was formed. Many members of the expedition stayed to live off the land by farming or ranching, and a permanent capital was founded at the town of Santa Fe.

The real task of building the colony was undertaken by the energetic padres. Determined to show the Indians the path to salvation, they established mission stations throughout the valley of the Rio Grande and the surrounding plains. The object of the padres' activity was the Pueblo Indians, who had a highly developed culture, lived in permanent villages, and practised agriculture. Their houses – called pueblos – were terraced buildings two or three storeys high, built of stone or adobe (mud bricks that are dried in the sun rather than fired in kilns). Their houses could be entered only by climbing ladders to the second floor; the ground storey was reached from above, and was solidly walled for protection from the Pueblos' enemies, the belligerent Ute and Comanche.

It was standard practice for a friar and a handful of Indian allies to cross the land on foot in search of a suitable Indian village in which to establish a new mission. Having selected a spot, the priest then began the process of converting the local

Indians: he instructed the natives in Christianity and in new methods of agriculture, helped them to build "proper" homes and a church, and taught them manual skills, arts, and crafts. In perhaps a decade a self-sufficient Christian agricultural village would be established. The friars would turn over the mission to the new parishioners and head out in search of yet another mission site. Their progress was astounding. By 1626 some forty-three churches had been built in New Mexico and, according to one friar, 34,000 Indians had been converted to Christianity (a number, however, larger than the entire estimated Pueblo Indian population).

The most magnificent of the New Mexico missions is San Estevan del Rey at Acoma. The fortress-like church sits atop a craggy sandstone mesa that rises some 350 feet above the surrounding land. For centuries the mesa had been the site of an Indian village, with closely packed terraced houses and with perhaps 3,000 inhabitants. Drinking water was trapped in natural reservoirs in the rock, but all food had to be carried up from the bottom by a difficult path cut into the jagged rock.

A party of Oñate's men visited Acoma in the fall of 1598 and were caught in a deadly surprise attack. In retaliation for the ambush, Oñate sent an armed force against the pueblo, which was razed completely. The conquered town was later rebuilt and priests were assigned to Christianize the Indians. The natives resisted conversion until after the arrival of Fray Juan Ramírez, a brave Franciscan who had taken holy orders in his native Mexico. Ramírez walked the one hundred miles from Sante Fe to Acoma, and in a short time won the trust and respect of the Indians. It was he who directed the building of the great church of San Estevan atop the mesa, only a short distance from the Indians' pueblo homes. The church was probably begun shortly after Ramírez's arrival in 1629, and was likely completed during the next fifteen years.

San Estevan church is a massive building, some 140 feet from end to end, with tapering walls that reach over thirty feet high and that in places are more than seven feet thick. Two bulky bell towers rise beside the entrance. Along one side is the *convento*, the home of the priest, with its rooms arranged around an enclosed patio.

The twin-towered façade and the basic proportions and arrangement of the church and *convento* were based on the appearance of a Mexican church of the sixteenth century, which in turn derived from the architecture of Spain. With each derivation from the Spanish model, the forms became simpler and the memory of Europe faded. San Estevan is utterly barren and austere; this may have been dictated partly by the need for an easily defended building – like the pueblos and like some Mexican fortress churches, it is almost impenetrable at ground level – but the explanation is more complex.

Father Ramírez, like the other New Mexico friars, designed the building himself. With no formal training in architecture, he remembered only the most significant features of the Mexican prototypes. His Indian flock erected the church in their traditional manner. The walls are built of adobe bricks, faced with field stone at the lower levels. To make the bricks, the Indians mixed natural clay with straw or manure, kneaded it with their bare feet or with hoes, tamped it into wooden boxes, and left it in the sun to dry. The roof was built by laying immense wooden beams called *vigas* – some as long as forty feet – across the nave. The *vigas* rest on gaily painted brackets (called "corbels") set into the walls. The beams were originally covered only with dirt and mud; today they are protected by a modern concrete slab.

Indian wall paintings inside San José, Laguna.

The spacious interior is equally impressive with its great white walls, pierced by few windows. Behind the altar is a bright mural painting that simulates the traditional carved reredos of the Spanish Roman Catholic churches. Its vertical division into three parts is similar to the typical *retable* of New France. The Pueblo Indians had a long tradition of mural painting in their ceremonial underground chambers [*kivas*]; the padres allowed them to continue this tradition here, adapting it to suit Christian worship.

San Estevan is a splendid monument, a testament to the strength of both the Spanish missionary organization and the Pueblo Indian culture. The power of the Catholic Church is obvious in the very existence of so great a church on top of the lonely New Mexico table rock. The Spanish architectural influence shows in all of the basic features of the church and its *convento*. Equally conspicuous is the Indian tradition: in the building materials and methods, the simplification of the Spanish forms, and the marvellous painted decoration. In most pioneer architecture a sophisticated tradition encountered primitive conditions and the meeting produced a new kind of building; here two accomplished architectural traditions came face to face and the result was a superb compromise.

The Indians did not accept Spanish rule complacently. Tensions built up over the years, and in 1680 the Indians rose against the Spaniards in a carefully organized Pueblo Revolt, killing or driving out most of the Spanish population. Many missions were destroyed.

One of the first missions founded after the Pueblo Revolt

At San José, Laguna, the floor of the choir loft is built of cedar poles laid in herring-bone fashion, a traditional Indian design.

was San José at Laguna, about fifteen miles northeast of Acoma. Friar Antonio Miranda formed the mission shortly before 1700, and the church and attached *convento* went up a few years later. The church is almost as long as San Estevan, but is somewhat narrower, lower, and more modest in appearance. Walls of rough stone (laid in adobe mortar) are plastered and white-washed to create the utterly austere appearance so characteristic of the New Mexico missions.

The façade provides the barest hint of a Spanish – or a Mexican – church. The curved profile of its summit recalls (with some imagination) the curved gables so loved by Spanish architects. The bells and the cross make the building identifiable as a church. Otherwise, the white walls with projecting *vigas* and the terraced composition look more like an Indian pueblo.

The mixture of Christian and pagan forms continues inside. As at Acoma, the end wall behind the altar is painted in imitation of a carved reredos. The side walls of the sanctuary are rampant with wild arabesques – a European art form – while the nave walls are painted from end to end with motifs drawn from traditional Pueblo religious art. A continuous band of hieroglyph-like figures includes the age-old Indian symbols for the sun, rain, and thunder. Overhead, a row of *vigas* is supported by brightly painted corbels. The floor of the choir loft, over the main entrance, is built of cedar poles laid herring-bone fashion, another traditional Indian design.

In other parts of the Spanish-American southwest, the native people possessed a weaker architectural tradition and as a result the Spanish style met less resistance. In Texas and Ari-

zona the mission churches look more like those of Mexico or of Spain. Unlike the New Mexican missions, which had been designed by the padres and built by the Indians, Texas missions were probably erected by professional Spanish builders and craftsmen. The Texas Indians were nomads with few permanent buildings of their own, and therefore offered little architectural input.

Texas was of little interest to the Spanish until the 1680s, when, fearing a French attack on New Spain, the government sent a military expedition to Texas. Four Franciscan missionaries under Father Damien Massanet accompanied the soldiers. Together they built a small mission outpost about one hundred miles northeast of today's Houston, Texas. Despite the presence of the post, however, France founded the colony of Louisiana. The Spanish belatedly retaliated by building a series of new missions across the Texas frontier to keep the French soldiers and traders away from their colony.

The finest of these missions is San José y San Miguel de Aguayo, built near San Antonio in the 1720s. The force behind the mission was Father Antonio Margil, a tireless administrator who was the padre *presidente* of the Franciscan mission field. The façade boasts two massive corner towers (somewhat like Acoma), one of which is capped by a large arched belfry. The walls are built of stuccoed tufa (a porous limestone) with brown sandstone used for trim. The most striking feature of the façade is the lavish carved stone frontispiece at the entrance, the work of Mexican sculptor Pedro Huizar. Around the openings of the door and oval window above it are statues of saints set into a profusely detailed architectural framework. The ornamental motifs such as foliage and scrolls — as well as their concentration around the doors and windows — derive from Spanish Baroque architecture and its seventeenth-century Mexican derivative. Other windows bear carved frames as well — perhaps the loveliest is that along the wall of the baptistry.

The mission field of Arizona was opened by Jesuits and extended by Franciscans. The Spanish made relatively little headway here, because the Indians remained quite hostile and few Spanish priests or farmers cared to settle there.

The Jesuits, too, were the first priests to work in the greatest of the Spanish-American mission fields, California. This territory included all of the undiscovered lands of the northwest. Jesuit priests founded a few settlements in Lower California around 1700, but never ventured north of the skinny peninsula. In 1767 King Charles III expelled the Jesuits from Spain and all Spanish dominions as part of a wave of hostility towards the Jesuits' wealth, influence, and discipline. The Jesuit missionaries of Lower California were seized "with no effects other than their clothing, breviaries, one theological and one historical book," and deported to the island of Corsica. In their place were left about a dozen earnest but apprehensive Franciscan missionaries who had been recruited from the College of San Fernando in Mexico City.

Their leader was a dedicated middle-aged priest named Junípero Serra, the president of the college and a veteran of mission work in Mexico and Texas. Serra's burning desire to Christianize the Indians of mainland California received complete support from the Spanish secular authorities. The king and his Mexican governors feared advances from the north by Russian fur traders, and also sought to establish a refitting point for galleons from across the Pacific.

Plans were struck to establish a series of missions along the California coast. Early in 1769 three ships and two land expeditions went north to the bay of San Diego. Only two of the ships arrived (the third was never seen again), and almost all of the passengers and crew aboard the other two vessels were dead or dying of scurvy. The survivors buried the dead, tended the sick, and pursued the business of establishing the missions.

On July 16, 1769, the fifty-six-year-old Serra raised a wooden cross, said mass, and dedicated the mission of San Diego de Alcalá — the first outpost of Christianity in California. The chapel was a shed made of poles thrust into the ground and covered with a grass roof. The momentous occasion was observed only by a handful of sick and hungry Spaniards, and by a group of curious Indians who watched from a safe distance in the nearby hills.

The Indians did not rush to seek conversion. Indeed, relations between the two races began most inauspiciously. Although the Indians would provide fish to the Spaniards for barter, they also stole almost everything portable — including clothes and bedsheets from the sick. Eventually the desperate soldiers opened fire, killing three Indians. It was to be several years before the first native was converted at San Diego.

After spending a miserable winter at San Diego, Father Serra left two priests and a small guard there and journeyed northward another 400 miles to the harbour of Monterey. In June 1770 Serra raised a second cross, hung a bell on an oak tree, and founded Mission San Carlos Borromeo. An "arbour of branches" served as a church until another structure could be built.

The Mission of San José y San Miguel de Aguayo, San Antonio.

Top and opposite: details of the elaborate carved stone frontispiece at San José y San Miguel de Aguayo. At the left is the main door of the mission; above is the baptistry window. All are the work of professional Spanish craftsmen, rather than Indians.

In the fourteen years that remained to him, the tireless Father Serra established seven more missions along the coast. He would make all of the arrangements for each new one, dedicate it, and leave it in the custody of two friars. One that gave him particular pleasure was Mission San Francisco de Asís, dedicated to the revered father of the Franciscan order. It was the first white settlement on the site of San Francisco, California.

Left: The nave of Mission San Diego de Alcalá is roofed with heavy timbers allegedly hauled by oxen sixty miles from the sierra. Above: the courtyard of the same mission.

After Father Serra's death in 1784 his work was continued by his ardent followers. Padre Fermín Francisco de Lasuén founded nine more missions, and his successors another three. In 1823 the chain was completed with the establishment of San Francisco Solano. Twenty-one missions lay along the 400-mile Camino Real – the King's Highway – from San Diego to San Francisco Bay, each separated by a day's journey of forty miles.

Each mission consisted of a number of buildings in which a large community lived and worked. Beside the mission's church was the *convento*, comprising the offices and dwellings of the padres. Further along were the living quarters for resident Indians, work rooms for the practice of industries and crafts, rooms for travellers (for the missions also served as inns), kitchens, and stables. All were usually built around an open patio and were connected by cloister-like arcaded corridors. Other Indians – as many as a few thousand – lived in a separate village a short distance from the mission compound.

The Indians had originally been attracted to the missions by the lure of gifts. As Father Juan Crespi, a colleague and contemporary of Serra, once remarked, "The Indians pay attention to and obey only those who give them something, and only by gifts and threats can they be attracted to progress, the catechism, or anything that pertains to the church." Neophytes who accepted baptism were fed, clothed, and instructed in religion and industry by the padres. Discipline was strict, and misbehaviour was harshly punished. At night the Indians were locked into the compound. Girls and single women were enclosed separately. Despite these rigid controls, the Indians enjoyed their new existence. After all, life was secure and the food was good.

Much more sophisticated architecturally than San Diego de Alcalá was the work that went into building the greatest of the California missions, San Juan Capistrano. In 1812 an earthquake left Capistrano a ruin, but the magnificent ivy-covered walls allow the visitor's imagination to reconstruct the mission's original grandeur. The church was begun in 1797 under the initiative of Padres Fuster and Santiago. Mexican stonemason Isidoro Aguilar directed the building of Capistrano, the only church in the string of missions to be built entirely of stone. The Indians eagerly participated in the great project. They quarried the yellow sandstone, hauled it six miles with the help of oxen, and erected the fine walls. The women – not normally a part of the California Indian labour force – wanted to share in the work. "Will the Lord be pleased if we bring small stones," they asked, "so that they may go into the walls?" The padres and their master mason agreed that he would, and the women and children joined the men at work.

The church's long nave was once covered by shallow domes of stone, and the transepts and choir by carefully fitted stone vaults. Door and window frames, columns, capitals, and mouldings were all carved with an elegance not matched anywhere else in California. A tall bell tower rose above the entrance.

In a fertile valley midway between San Juan Capistrano and San Diego stands the mission of San Luís Rey de Francia, dedicated to Louis IX, king of France. Founded in 1798, the mission was the last established by Serra's energetic successor, Padre Lasuén. The large church, the mission's second, was begun in 1811 under the direction of Padre Antonio Peyri, who is said to have had some training in architecture. Its abundant arches and domes are characteristic of the buildings of Spain and Mexico, but are curiously absent in so many of the pioneer missions in the southern American Plains. The handsome façade is a more elaborate version of San Diego, with a similar decoratively curved gable at the top. The crisply carved door frame and the large pilasters embracing the whole façade reflect the neoclassical architecture that was the vogue in Europe. A pair of towers flank the façade; the one on the right is topped by a two-staged domed belfry. The walls of San Luís Rey are built of adobe and faced with brick and stucco. The wall trim is brick. The roofs are covered with moulded red Spanish tile.

The central portion of the façade shares many of the features of Quebec parish churches, such as Notre-Dame-des-Victoires or Saint-François-de-Sales: for example, tall proportions, the same kind of door, and a circular window neatly

balanced by three sculpted niches. Franciscans in opposite corners of the new continent reproduced just enough of their European heritage – in one place conveyed through Spanish forms and in the other through French – to preserve the family resemblance.

The impressive nave of San Luís Rey is divided into sections by pilasters painted to simulate marble. These branch out into broad arches at the crossing. Timber roof beams rest on corbels and cover the nave, while a lovely wooden dome rises above the crossing.

The construction of San Luís Rey in 1811-1815 coincided with the missions' peak of prosperity. In that same decade Mexico began its revolution against Spanish rule, finally de-

Right and opposite: The courtyard of San Luís Rey de Francia, showing the residential and working quarters of the compound.

claring its independence in 1821. California became Mexican, but in the subsequent period of unsteady rule the missions were without any government support at all. Indians who had been in the missions for some time were permitted by law to leave. The arrival of the American pioneers set an example of a new kind of freedom that further reduced the influence of the padres. The final blow came with the secularization of the missions in 1834. Within two years all missions were in the hands of civil trustees, and much of their land was distributed among the natives. The Indians, in turn, sold their new property and quickly spent the proceeds. Remaining mission lands were disposed of in the 1840s. Only Mission Santa Barbara stayed in Franciscan hands.

The American government claimed California in 1846. After the initial frontier phase, Californians began to look with romantic delight at the old mission buildings. Most had fallen into decay, and some were totally ruined. A number of missions had found ignominious new lives as stables or saloons. Toward the end of the last century Californians began to preserve and restore the ruins. San Juan Capistrano, for example, was returned to the Catholic Church in 1865 and repaired a bit, and in 1896 the Landmarks Club — an early preservationist group — took a lease on it and began to stabilize the ruins. San Diego de Alcalá was turned over to the church in 1862, and serious restoration was carried out in 1931. And so it was with most of the mission buildings.

The English Settlers:
The Anglicans
and the South

The English effort to colonize North America focused on the central part of the eastern seaboard. Like the French to the north and the Spanish to the south, the English colonists were accompanied by clergymen. But unlike their Catholic brethren, the Anglican missionaries conceived their duty to be more to their English parishioners than to the natives.

In 1606 James I granted a royal charter to a group of English merchants known as the Virginia Company, authorizing them to "make habitation, plantation, and to deduce a colony of sundry of our people into that part of America commonly called Virginia." This name, chosen to honour the virgin Queen Elizabeth, was used to describe most of the eastern seaboard of North America, specifically that between the thirty-fourth and forty-fifth parallels of latitude – from today's Charleston, South Carolina, to Halifax, Nova Scotia. The southern part of this territory was the responsibility of a division of the Virginia Company known as the London Company.

In the spring of 1607, three tiny London Company ships, the *Susan Constant*, the *Godspeed*, and the *Discovery*, cruised under reduced sail into the calm waters of Chesapeake Bay. The 105 gentlemen and labourers who crowded their decks marvelled at the surrounding fields ablaze with wild flowers. They were particularly grateful for the numerous streams and rivers of fresh water; after months of shipboard rationing, a plentiful supply of water was a godsend. The ships entered the mouth of a river which the expedition's leaders christened the James, in honour of their king. Proceeding upstream, the party anchored at a marshy peninsula, disembarked, and began to build houses and a protective palisade. This was James Fort, later to become the nucleus of Jamestown, in the present state of Virginia. It was the first successful English foothold in North America.

The business of building the colony was agonizingly slow. In September, four months after their landing, Captain John Smith, the settlers' leader, wrote, "as yet we had no houses to cover us, our Tents were rotten, and our Cabbins worse than nought."

Smith had been charged with seeing that "the true word, and service of God and Christian faith be preached, planted and used . . . according to the . . . religion now professed and established within our realme of England." Attendance at Sunday services was compulsory.

At first an old sail was hung on some trees to shelter the worshippers from the sun. As work on the houses and palisade progressed, a proper church was begun. As Smith recalled, "we built a homely thing like a barne, set upon Cratchets, covered with rafts, sedge and earth; so also was the walls." The word "Cratchets" probably refers to cruck frame construction, a traditional method then common in parts of England. In a cruck frame, pairs of curved or bent tree trunks are joined together to form an inverted "V", which is raised upright on a foundation or is planted in the ground. The system produces a series of pointed arches – called "cruck trusses" – to which the roofing and walls are attached.

For centuries this system had been used in England to frame houses and, as Smith notes, barns – although not churches, which usually had walls of masonry. Most English crucks were no more than twenty feet high. The tallest one known, a barn in Worcestershire, is over thirty feet in height. The old-country roofing may often have been thatch, a closely woven mat of plant materials, usually straw or reed. In Virginia the settlers used "sedge"– probably rushes or reeds gathered from the river bank. Earth and wood ("rafts") made up for the other traditional materials not at hand.

The Jamestown pioneers clung to the traditions they had learned in England, but when conditions dictated a new approach, they found an expedient solution. The pioneers did not invent – they adapted. The success of any colony was a measure of its inhabitants' adaptability.

In addition to poor crops, lack of supplies, and rampant disease during the first year, a disastrous fire levelled every building so painstakingly erected in the settlement. Shortly after the fire, the Jamestown pioneers built a second church. It, too, must have been quickly put together, for it was already "ruined and unfrequented" in 1610 when Sir Thomas West, Baron De la Warr (for whom the state of Delaware was eventually named), arrived to take up his duties as the Virginia Company's governor. He restored this second church, described by a contemporary observer as "a pretty chapel . . . in length 60 feet, in breadth 24, . . . with a chancel of cedar and a communion table of black walnut; all the pews and pulpit were of cedar, with bare broad windows, also of cedar, shut and opened, as the weather shall occasion. . . . There were two bells in the steeple at the west end. The Church was so cast as to be very light within, and the Lord Governour caused it to be kept passing sweet and well trimmed up with diverse flowers."

The church has been reconstructed with a frame of squared timbers and with a steeply-gabled thatched roof. The spaces between the wooden posts and beams were packed with masonry or with wattle (tightly interlaced twigs) – the "half-timber" construction of Tudor England. The Jamestown settlers again used traditional forms, adapting them where necessary to indigenous materials.

As the Virginia plantation owners bought up the land and brought over indentured servants, the colony expanded rapidly

First Church, Jamestown, Virginia (Forman: *The Architecture of the Old South*, 1948).

Cruck-frame barn of Wigmore Abbey, Herefordshire, engraved by Le Keux (1871).

throughout the tidewater regions of Virginia and the adjacent colony of Maryland. Parishes were established and churches built. Major concentrations of settlers, such as those in Jamestown, had their own churches. Outlying parishes later received churches. Wherever a cluster of farms was too remote to be served adequately by a church, a more conveniently located "chapel of ease" was constructed, in which visiting vicars or local readers might officiate.

A fine example of a parish church of this period is Merchant's Hope Church, which originally sat amidst some large plantations in Prince George County, a region south of the James River settled soon after Jamestown. The church takes its quaint name from the old plantation on which it stood. (The plantation was named either for a ship that brought many English colonists to Virginia in 1634 and 1635, or for Martin's Hope – pronounced similarly in the archaic dialect – the name of the property held in 1620 by Captain John Martin.) In 1656 a local merchant willed the parish a fund for construction and repair of a church. The church was probably built the following year. The date 1657 is carved into one of its massive rafters.

Merchant's Hope is a modest structure, about the same size and shape as the second Jamestown church, and is typical of the smaller seventeenth-century Virginia parish churches. The half-timbered construction used in the second Jamestown church has been translated here into more permanent brick. A steeply gabled roof sweeps into a gentle curve at the eaves. The building's simplicity – the rigid rectangular form unbroken with porch, bell tower, or other addition – resembles the early churches of other North American pioneers. Its shape and bell-cast eaves are similar, for example, to those of Notre-Dame-des-Victoires or Saint-François on the Ile d'Orléans. Similar pioneer conditions led to similar simplified architectural responses. Nevertheless the proportions of the Virginia church appear to be more squat – less vertical – than those of the Quebec ones, suggesting a difference between the English and the French eyes for design.

Predictably, the internal arrangement of Merchant's Hope Church follows the traditional form of the English parish church that the Virginia settlers would have known. The nave is entered by the main door on the western end of the building;

the eastern chancel is entered by a door on one of the longer sides. Tall windows along both sides illuminate the nave, while the smaller window above the main entrance lights the gallery. The rounded window heads, the brick arches, the finely crafted window sashes and frames, the cornice beneath the eaves that incorporates small decorative brackets ("modillions") – all these details display the forms and the attention to fine craftsmanship found in seventeenth-century England.

All the earliest buildings of Virginia had been constructed of wood and temporary materials. Unfortunately, no early wood buildings have survived in the moist Virginia climate. By mid-century, brick began to be preferred for more important structures. Many of the settlers had come from eastern and southern England, where brick buildings were common.

A handsome brick structure that originally resembled Merchant's Hope Church is St. Peter's Church in New Kent County, Virginia. Surviving vestry records relate that St. Peter's was erected between 1701 and 1703 under the direction of William Hughes, a carpenter:

> Whereas the Lower Church of this parish is very much out of Repair and Standeth very inconvenient for most of the inhabitants of the said parish. Therefore ordered that as soon as conveniently may be a new Church of Brick Sixty feet long and twenty fower feet wide in the Cleer and fourteen feet pitch with a Gallery Sixteen feet Long be built and Erected upon the maine Roade by the School House near Thomas Jackson's; and the Clark is ordered to give a Copy of This order to Capt. Nicho. Merewether who is Requested to show the same to Will Hughes and desire him to draw a Draft of the said Church.

The parishioners knew that this was all the instruction that was necessary to achieve the design they wanted. Hughes produced the "draft" and built the church, a towerless brick rectangle. The gables at either end project above the roof as a parapet, as do those at the Old Brick Church mentioned in the Introduction. The gables of St. Peter's are curved (the Old Brick Church's are stepped) in a modern and plausible restoration based on other early Virginian buildings. This kind of gable – usually termed Flemish or Jacobean – was common in southeastern England. A belfry was added over the west end of St. Peter's in 1722. In addition to its function of summoning worshippers, the bell tower is a sign of the fact that by this time the people were "dressing up" their basic house of worship. The present tower was raised about 1742 and every parishioner was tithed five pounds of tobacco to help pay for it.

On January 6, 1759, St. Peter's was the setting for the marriage of a prominent Virginia planter, George Washington, to the widow Martha Dandridge Custis. To commemorate this historic connexion, the General Assembly of Virginia has designated St. Peter's as "The First Church of the First First-Lady."

In 1699 the capital of Virginia was transferred from Jamestown to Williamsburg in Bruton Parish after another fire damaged Jamestown. The church then standing in Williamsburg was soon recognized as inadequate for the newly enlarged congregation and its many royal functions. Since 1624 the governors of Virginia had been appointed by the crown, which invested the office with much pomp and ceremony. The existing church in Bruton Parish was described by its vestry (or church administration) in 1706 as being in "bad condition"; four years later it was deemed "ruinous." The vestry asked the House of

St. James' Church at Goose Creek, South Carolina, was built by Anglican plantation owners from Barbados at the beginning of the eighteenth century.

Burgesses for financial aid to help them with a new church. Not only did they get some money, but they also received a building plan. In 1711 Governor Alexander Spotswood gave the rector of Bruton Parish "a platt or draught of a Church (whose length is 75 foot and bredth 28 foot in the clear with two wings on each side, whose width is 22 foot) which he laid before the Vestry for approbation – Adding further that the Honble the Governor proposed to the Vestry to build only 53 of the 75 foot, and that he would take care for the remaining part." The vestry happily accepted.

The Bruton Parish Church was one of the first Anglican churches in North America to incorporate transepts – rectangular projections along the sides (the "wings" of Governor Spotswood's plan) – as part of the original building. In England this cruciform plan was the rule rather than the exception; in Virginia, smaller and less affluent congregations created a reverse situation.

At the east end of Bruton Parish Church is situated the chancel, that part of the church reserved for the clergy. The altar stands within the chancel; here the priest celebrates the Eucharist. Before the altar extends the communion rail at which worshippers may kneel to receive the sacrament. Along the south wall beyond the chancel, at a point where the south transept intersects with the nave, rises the pulpit with a sounding

board above it and a reading desk below. From the pulpit the sermon was preached; from the desk the prayers were read. The pulpit and desk were placed, by Anglican tradition, so that the congregation could better hear both the sermon and the prayers, which had been delivered in English since the Reformation. The chancel was enlarged in 1752 to accommodate the organ, usually located at the opposite end.

Even this, the Chapel Royal of Virginia, was originally built without a tower. The present steeple was added in 1769 to house the "Liberty Bell of Virginia," as it was dubbed after announcing to the countryside the signing in Philadelphia of the Declaration of Independence.

One of the most delightful of southern pioneer churches is St. James' Church at Goose Creek, South Carolina. South Carolinians were granted freedom of worship, but in 1706 the Church of England was named as the established church: while a person could worship as he saw fit, his taxes paid for the construction and upkeep of Anglican churches and for the Anglican clergy's salary. Behind this move was a determined group of Anglicans from the Barbados. They had settled at Goose Creek in 1685, lured by the promise that a new settler who was also a slave owner would have "absolute Power and Authority over his Negro Slaves," and that the Anglican Church would be publicly supported.

Inside St. James' Church are columns of solid pine and an elaborate reredos. The pulpit has been placed in the chancel with the altar.

The Barbadians' first church building was of wood. The present St. James' was built between 1708 and 1719. The plan is almost square – more so than the Virginia churches of the same period. The brick walls and the decorative quoins at the corners are covered with stucco in a fashion similar to West Indian Spanish-influenced buildings. St. James' is an English church twice removed; once by the island frontier and once again by the American mainland.

The church's pioneer simplicity is nicely complemented by sophisticated classical detail. Around the main entrance, two Doric pilasters support a horizontal panel (a triglyph frieze) and a triangular pediment. Flaming hearts decorate the frieze and the stucco heads of cherubs smile above the arched windows.

Inside the church the worshipper faces an unusually elaborate reredos. Pairs of Corinthian pilasters, made of stucco and painted to imitate marble, support a large broken pediment which bears the arms of George I. The arch above the central window contains lettering and two cherubs holding a Bible. Later in the eighteenth century the tablets with texts were placed over the pilasters, and the present pulpit was inserted into the chancel together with the altar, creating a single liturgical centre.

Two rows of solid pine columns imitate the division of larger English churches into nave and side aisles. To further the illusion, the ceiling is raised higher in the centre to make it look like a proper nave. Planks cut with an arched underside are inserted between the tops of the columns to simulate vaulting above the aisles.

The modest little building with its decorated chancel, solid columns, and imitation vaulting aspired to the dignity of a grand three-aisled church in England, an aspiration explained by the carved pelican that sits in the pediment above the main entrance. The pelican was the emblem of the Society for the Propagation of the Gospel in Foreign Parts (SPG), an Anglican missionary organization founded in 1701, which dispatched a representative to Goose Creek in the following year. The rector who supervised construction of the church, Dr. Francis Le Jau, was an SPG missionary. St. James' was the centre of the religious activism of the Goose Creek men, and it was essential to them that their church be identified with the recently established society.

While the English settlers in the southern colonies were predominantly Anglicans, loyal to the tenets of the church as practised in the homeland, in the north the settlers were mostly members of dissident denominations that questioned Anglican dogma and liturgy. As a result, when the northern pioneers built their houses of worship, they were very different from the churches erected by their southern cousins.

THE SECOND CHURCH, JAMESTOWN, VIRGINIA

In 1610, when Lord De La Warr repaired its second church, Jamestown stood at the western edge of English settlement in the Virginia colony. Tobacco plantations were springing up along the James River and tension was mounting between the colonists and hostile Indian tribes. Four years later, the Englishman John Rolfe married the celebrated Indian princess Pocahontas in this church. Pocahontas's father, Powhatan, supposedly agreed to the alliance to create goodwill between his people and the settlers; but some historians insist that she was captured by the English to ensure the good behaviour of the Indians.

The attempt at peace-making was short-lived. After Powhatan died, a more militant chieftain named Opechancanough led the Indians in an attack. In 1622 more than three hundred settlers were slaughtered and all of the isolated plantations were destroyed. The colonists were quick to retaliate and their reprisals, coupled with the increase in numbers of settlers, gradually quelled the Indians' attacks.

Pocahontas was immortalized as the heroine of Captain John Smith's *Historie of Virginia, New-England and the Summer Isles*. As reported in Ben Jonson's *The Staple of Newes*, she was the object of considerable curiosity when received in 1616 by King James I as a fellow monarch. She was, however, soon abandoned by admirers and died neglected and impoverished a year later.

Her husband's method of curing tobacco rendered the Virginia crop exportable, providing an income-producing industry for the colony.

The original Second Church, like many of its generation, did not survive the ravages of time. The present church (shown on this and the opposite page) was reconstructed on the site.

EARLY VIRGINIA CHURCHES

The earliest buildings of Virginia were constructed of wood and other temporary materials. By mid-century, brick began to be preferred for more important structures. Many of the settlers had come from eastern and southern England, where brick buildings were most common. Among them were a number of bricklayers and brickmakers. They found an abundant local supply of clay, and they took lime for mortar from the oyster shells that were plentiful along the shore. Wooden

Opposite: despite its extreme simplicity, there is an aristocratic mien to the little Merchant's Hope Church, Prince George County, Virginia. Above: the somewhat later church of St. Peter, New Kent County, Virginia, has an air of monumentality akin to that of English parish churches.

churches were still built in large numbers, but no early ones have survived. Those that were not burned or demolished were destroyed by the moist Virginia climate.

Two of the loveliest Virginia brick churches of the pioneers are Merchant's Hope Church, Prince George County (opposite), and St. Peter's Church in New Kent County (above). The eye-catching tower of St. Peter's was erected forty years after the church was built, at the beginning of the eighteenth century.

It was in St. Peter's that George Washington married the widow Martha Dandridge Custis on January 6, 1759. The newlyweds spent a leisurely honeymoon at the bride's nearby residence, then made their home at Washington's estate at Mount Vernon. In a few years, Washington was commandeered as military leader of the colonial forces in the Revolutionary War.

OLD TRINITY CHURCH, CHURCH CREEK, MARYLAND

Old Trinity (opposite and above) is a charming, intimate brick church built around 1675 on an inlet of Chesapeake Bay. It has undergone many alterations over the years, but was restored to its original state in the 1950s. It is only thirty-eight feet by twenty feet in size. The walkway and the interior floor of the church are made of bricks.

During the restoration project, heart pine was salvaged from old homes in Pennsylvania, Virginia, and Maryland for the construction of the pews. Family privacy is maintained by doors that enclose the pews; before the days of central heating, the doors afforded a means of keeping in warmth.

On the north wall is a reproduction of the original three-decked pulpit. The railing and altar table in the apse are made from native black walnut; the elaborate seventeenth-century chandelier that hangs before them is made of brass.

A Table of Marriages hangs on the back wall inside the church. A mandatory feature of all Episcopal churches at the time, the table provided lists of all relatives a man or woman could not marry.

Maryland, originally settled by Catholics disgusted with the intolerance of the time, has been proud of its history of complete religious tolerance. Old Trinity has always remained open to all denominations as a place of worship. Until 1692 it was obliged – along with many other colonial churches –to pay tithes to the Bishop of London, but during the reign of Queen Anne it was granted full privileges as an independent church. She issued two orders in 1703 that provided the church with a Bible, Communion Service, and a personal gift – a beautiful cushion on which she had knelt at her coronation.

THE BRUTON PARISH CHURCH, WILLIAMSBURG, VIRGINIA

Whoever made the plans for Bruton Parish Church (shown on this page and opposite), it is clear that he had social hierarchy in mind when he laid out the seating arrangements. The colony's governor, Alexander Spotswood, and his Council of State (an appointed advisory group) occupied an elevated pew close by the pulpit and facing it. This vice-regal pew was draped with a red velvet canopy that carried in gold the name of the governor – a name that was changed for each incumbent. Members of the House of Burgesses (elected by their peers, and nowadays pointed out as the oldest regularly sitting elected governing group in the English-speaking world) sat in pews arranged in the transepts. The Speaker of the House and parishioners of wealth and distinction were assigned pews in the gallery of the north transept. The rest of the congregation occupied the handsome panelled box pews in the nave – women on the south side and men on the north, as was the custom. Students of the College of William and Mary were relegated to the western gallery. Today the church is part of restored Williamsburg, one of the attractions in that elaborate re-creation of colonial America, which was made possible by John D. Rockefeller.

OLD MEETING HOUSE, HARPSWELL CENTER, MAINE

The meeting houses of New England amalgamate two architectural sources: the English parish church and the English town hall. From the former the Puritans borrowed the idea of a rectangular hall with the pulpit on one side opposite a door; from the latter they took many of the external features: the hipped roof, the balustraded platform, and the crowning turret. There being no developed form of non-conformist architecture known to the Puritan settlers, they fell back on known models, as did settlers on every frontier across North America. Up and down the New England coast the style born of these two unlikely parents flourished into the eighteenth century.

An attractive survival of this style is the Old Meeting House at Harpswell Center, Maine, which dates from 1757-1759. After the inhospitable climate had defeated the first settlers at Fort St. George (just to the east of Harpswell Center) in 1607, settlement of the northern coast proceeded slowly. Congregationalism became the established religion in Maine, so much so that in 1715 a group of developers surveying prospective Maine town-sites made a proposal that read:

> Being desirous that the people may not live like
> Heathen, without worship of God, as has been too
> frequent in new Settlements, as soon as there shall be
> to the Number of twenty Householders in each of Sd
> Townes, the said Inhabitants providing a Frame for
> a Meeting House, and raising of it, we will at our Ex-
> pense furnish for the meeting house in each Town
> Glass, Lead, Nails, Iron work and other Materials,
> and to finish it for them.

So linked were church and state that the congregations elected the ministers and the towns paid their salaries. In Brunswick, Maine, near Harpswell Center, fully three-quarters of the taxes collected went toward the minister's salary. When this system worked well, it worked very well indeed; when it failed, as it did during the notorious witch trials at Salem, Massachusetts, it bore dire consequences.

The meeting house at Harpswell Center was the community's first. The small, clapboarded frame building was probably built by carpenter Elisha Eaton, son of the first pastor. The architecture is austere; no superfluous ornament detracts from its simplicity.

After the erection of a new church in 1844, the Old Meeting House was used only for town meetings. The centre pews have been removed, but otherwise the interior survives virtually unaltered. Even the original plasterwork remains in good condition.

OLD SHIP MEETING HOUSE, HINGHAM, MASSACHUSETTS

The New England meeting house was intended as a place of intimate worship. Old Ship Meeting House (on this page and opposite) is an excellent example of the form. The pulpit was placed along the longer wall to bring the preacher into the closest possible contact with his congregation. While Anglican churches had chancels from which the minister would serve communion, Puritans omitted this feature. The *sacrificial* nature of communion was paramount in the Anglican service – the communicant knelt to receive the sacrament at the altar rail; but the *communal* aspect of the Last Supper was emphasized by the Puritans – the communicant remained in his seat for the ritual. Social status was also indicated by the seating arrangement. Women sat to the minister's left, men to his right, and the higher the prestige of the member the nearer the pulpit he sat. Black servants and converted Indians were relegated to the most remote pews. The meeting house was the setting in which the prophecy of John Winthrop, the Puritan leader, was to be shaped: "Men shall say of succeeding generations: 'The Lord make it like that of New England.' "

THE MEETING HOUSE, SANDOWN, NEW HAMPSHIRE

Erected between the years 1773 and 1774, this fine meeting house at Sandown, New Hampshire (on this page and opposite), preserves unspoiled the beauty of simple materials and thoughtful workmanship. Built when the colonies were on the very brink of the Revolutionary War, the Sandown meeting house does not occupy an honoured place on the main street of the village. Instead it is located on a quiet hilltop at the geographical centre of the township of Sandown. Placing the church here achieved a kind of abstract perfection that suited the God-centred New England community. An *Essay on the ordering of towns*, written about 1635, underscores this idea:

> First, Suppose the Toune Square 6 miles every waye.
> The Houses orderly placed about the midst, especially
> the Meeting house, the which we will suppose to be the
> Centor of the wholl Circomference.

When these towns were originally laid out, the builders would have constructed in the familiar English tradition, raising the high-pitched gables and half-timbering of a post-Tudor English village. It took only a few winters and summers on the east coast of America to see that England could not be transplanted to America without adaptation and change. Shrinking wood, cracking wattle-and-daub, draughts, and dampness drove uncomfortable settlers to cover their homes and public buildings with boards which overlapped, now known as clapboards. The special look of New England began with this need for the protection of wind- and weather-proof wood.

The white clapboard look came later. Early in the pioneer era, it was not unusual to see unpainted structures; when they were painted, the colour was often Spanish brown and other sombre earth colours. Much later on, skimmed milk and buttermilk were used as a paint medium, as well as lime whitewash.

ST. MARY'S ANGLICAN CHURCH, AUBURN, NOVA SCOTIA

St. Mary's Anglican Church (opposite) was built in 1790 in the centre of the fertile and attractive Annapolis valley, not far from the site of Port Royal, the first permanent French settlement in Canada. The valley was originally the home of Acadians, French colonists whose property was ceded by France to Britain in 1713. After the Acadians were banished from Nova Scotia in 1755, New England farmers—Anglicans and dissenters alike – were invited to take over the land. Within a few years about 45,000 New Englanders came to the province; more arrived as United Empire Loyalists after the American Revolutionary War. Today the valley is still farmed, and produces some of the finest apples in the continent.

St. Mary's is very much an English church, built by Anglicans as a kind of smaller version of St. Paul's in Halifax or

Above: details of the Sandown Meeting House, described on the previous page. Opposite: this view of St. Mary's Church, Auburn, Nova Scotia, from the south reveals the distinctive touch of its Anglican builders.

Trinity in Newport. Master builder William Matthews built the frame out of pine trees that were felled and sawn nearby, and the timbers are held together with wooden pins. The narrow clapboard siding, which looks so much as if it had been built in New England, was fastened with hand-forged nails that had been brought from Halifax. James Morden, Ordnance Storekeeper of Halifax, gave six acres of land for the church on the condition that one pew be kept for him and his heirs forever. Pew number eight is still marked with his name.

Backed by a grove of trees and surrounded by old gravestones, St. Mary's simple lines and harmonious proportions create a lovely image of serenity.

St. Mary's Church was built at the end of an era. Its distinctly English form was by now a rarity on a continent where the various denominations and sects had gradually blended their building styles so that they were often indistinguishable. After the turn of the century, at the end of two centuries of settlement along the east coast, the meeting houses of the dissenters and the churches of the Anglicans were beginning to look very much alike. They created a new tradition of wood construction which was·to be carried across the continent.

THE OLD COVENANTERS' CHURCH, HORTON, NOVA SCOTIA

American Congregationalists who immigrated to Nova Scotia faced a number of problems. There was a shortage of clergymen, and the region was further beset by divisions within its own ranks. At Grand Pré, Nova Scotia, the resident Congregationalists (mostly from Rhode Island and Connecticut) changed the old Acadian name, Grand Pré, to Horton. The only pastor available was an Irish Presbyterian from New Jersey. With the adaptability that is the hallmark of successful colonists everywhere, the Horton settlers took their pastor's faith.

The free intermixing of dissenting sects was not uncommon on the frontier.

The Horton meeting house, which later became known as the Old Covenanters' Church (opposite and above), was built between 1804 and 1811. It could be mistaken for a New England Congregationalist meeting house of a century earlier. Originally it was of the familiar type, five windows wide, with the upper windows tucked tightly under the narrow eaves. The tower was added about a dozen years later, allegedly because the local Methodists had just completed a church with a steeple and the Congregationalists-turned-Presbyterians were not to be outdone.

THE MEETING HOUSE, BARRINGTON, NOVA SCOTIA

One group of forty Congregationalist families from Cape Cod received a grant of 100,000 acres at Barrington, near the southern tip of Nova Scotia. In 1761 they loaded their household goods and livestock aboard a small fleet of boats and sailed the 250 miles to their new home. A year later they were joined by the families of whalers from Nantucket. It was a move fraught with hardships and uncertainty, a move from the tried and familiar to the unexpected. But the settlers knew that they were going to a land that had been broken and cultivated, a land where, as they subsequently found out, the British connection was more firmly rooted than it was in New England.

By 1765 the Barrington settlers were ready to build their meeting house. The plain structure (above and opposite) is similar in size, proportion, and design to the meeting houses of most New England towns; it differs very little, for example, from that at Harpswell Center. After all, the settlers were New Englanders and their first pastor, Samuel Wood, was a Harvard graduate from Connecticut.

At the time, neither Barrington nor any nearby town boasted a sawmill, so it is likely that the timbers for the meeting house frame were shipped from Boston.

Nova Scotia and Massachusetts were, of course, both colonies of Britain. Only later, after the Revolutionary War, did the political distinction between them begin to matter. When the Declaration of Independence was proclaimed in 1776, the citizens of Maugerville wrote to George Washington, asking him to conquer Nova Scotia. He never attempted to.

After the American-British peace treaty of 1783, many Americans who remained loyal to the British Crown chose to leave the new republic and settle in the English colonies. Some fled as political refugees, while others were moved by a more passive desire to remain under the British flag. These United Empire Loyalists settled in the existing colonies of Nova Scotia (part of which became New Brunswick) and Prince Edward Island, and also trudged further west to the upper St. Lawrence River and the Great Lakes regions. These Loyalists who fled to the northern colonies were Tory in politics and mostly Anglican in religion. Canadian history books say little or nothing about the settlers who opted for republican government and headed south; and most Americans are hardly aware of the large numbers of people who chose not to join the forces for revolution, but headed north instead.

ST. EDWARD'S CHURCH, CLEMENTSPORT, NOVA SCOTIA

A group of United Empire Loyalists reached Clementsport, in the Annapolis Basin, in 1784. Six years later, Bishop Charles Inglis of Nova Scotia wrote to the Society for the Propagation of the Gospel in London that the "inhabitants of Clements, amounting to fifty families and mostly Loyalists had petitioned the government for money to build a church." Resident Dowie Ditmars sold the church a plot of land high on a hill, overlooking the water, for "one pepper corn." The timber for the church was felled on the site, and the building (left and below) was completed in 1795. It is now used as a museum, and services are held in it only once a year.

Not far away, at Tusket, Yarmouth County, stands a cairn dedicated to the United Empire Loyalists. The inscription reads, "They sacrificed everything save honour." A United Empire Loyalist was, according to Sir Guy Carleton, Lord Dorchester, governor-in-chief of British North America, any of the 50,000 or so immigrants who had left the Thirteen Colonies between 1776 and 1783. Those who came later were called "late Loyalists." In 1789 Sir Guy directed that true Loyalists, as "a Marke of Honor," might "be distinguished by the letters U.E. affixed to their names." The letters stood for "Unity of the Empire."

In spite of the sacrifice noted on the Loyalist cairn at Tusket, most Loyalists who came up from the Atlantic colonies and setled in the Maritimes fared better than the Loyalists who came from New York and Pennsylvania and settled in Ontario. In general, the Loyalists who came to Upper Canada (as the region west of Quebec was known) from the inland American colonies moved from one set of pioneer conditions to another. In the Maritimes, the Loyalists came from settled cities and towns and established farms to similar circumstances north of the border.

WEST PARISH MEETING HOUSE, WEST BARNSTABLE, MASSACHUSETTS

The meeting house built in 1717 at West Barnstable on Cape Cod (on this page and opposite) carries on the covenant established in 1616 in Southwark, England, by the first group to be designated Congregationalists. Forced by persecutors to leave England, the group came to New England in 1634, bringing with them sacramental vessels filled with church records, which are still kept at West Parish.

The meeting house suffered a nineteenth-century remodelling, but was restored in 1953 to its original elegance. The high pulpit and sounding board, the galleries, and the stairs referred to in old records were located by following scars and markings on the walls. The half-ton bell, cast on commission by Paul Revere & Son in 1803, was retained. It still summons the congregation to worship. The building's tall tower, capped by a cupola and weather cock, shows the tendency to make some meeting houses look more like churches.

ST. PAUL'S, HALIFAX, NOVA SCOTIA

Halifax was founded in 1749 by His Majesty's Board of Trade and Plantations. It was carefully planned on paper by engineers and surveyors in order to fulfil the function of a British military base; the town was meant to counterbalance the French fortress at Louisbourg on nearby Cape Breton Island. When naming Halifax, it was decided to honour the Board of Trade's president George Junk, who also happened to be the Earl of Halifax; the board chose to use his title rather than his family name.

When planning the layout of the town, a prominent site was chosen for the Anglican church, a building which Governor Edward Cornwallis hoped would combine the best in English design with the most expert North American craftsmanship. Cornwallis arranged to bring plans for St. Paul's from England to Boston, where the frame was to be built and then shipped to Halifax. The Reverend William Tutty, the first rector of St. Paul's, had been sent to Halifax by the Society for the Propagation of the Gospel. He speculated that the church "now framing at Boston" would be "capable of holding 900 persons." Both Tutty and Cornwallis were delighted by St. Paul's similarity to James Gibbs' design for Marylebone Chapel (the original name for St. Peter's, Vere Street, in London). Tutty wrote enthusiastically, "it is exactly the model of Mary'bone Chapel." Cornwallis assured his superiors of the church's propriety: "I expect the Frame of the Church will be here next month from New England, the plan is the same with that of Marybone Chapel."

The armed forces that built Halifax were very nearly the cause of its destruction when, on December 6, 1917, the Norwegian ship, *Imo,* collided with the ammunition vessel, *Mont Blanc.* It resulted in the death and injury of thousands of people and the levelling of hundreds of buildings; but the designers and builders of St. Paul's had done their job well. While newer buildings crumbled around it, the church stood firmly and was declared the only safe sanctuary in the town.

St. Paul's has been greatly altered over the years: aisles have been appended along the sides, a chancel added at the rear, and all the windows replaced. Fifty years after its original construction, a heating system was installed. Two stoves were originally intended to provide heat, but they smoked so badly that they could not be used. Parishioners brought foot warmers to church in winter – iron boxes filled with burning charcoal or wooden boxes with heated bricks inside; some worshippers even brought their dogs for warmth. The wooden clapboard that was first sawn in Halifax and then nailed to the oak and pine timbers from Boston are now heavily painted, and imitation quoins were placed at the corners of the building and around the windows to simulate stone. The old view of St. Paul's at left (drawn by R. Short, painted by D. Serres, and engraved by J. Fougeron) shows the east entrance of the church during an army parade in Halifax.

TRINITY CHURCH, NEWPORT, RHODE ISLAND

The first Church of England parish north of the Mason-Dixon line was King's Chapel, founded in Boston in 1683. There followed in quick succession Christ Church in Philadelphia, 1695; Trinity Church in New York, 1696; and Trinity Church in Newport (opposite and above) in 1698.

The Revocation of the Edict of Nantes in 1685 drove many prominent Huguenot families from France to the New World. The religious freedom of Rhode Island appealed to many of these persecuted Protestants. Their ritualistic leanings, along with a profound reaction to the excesses of Puritanism (which had resulted in Salem's witchcraft panic of 1692), moved them to join with the handful of English colonists loyal to the less extreme forms of Protestant worship.

They organized the parish of Trinity Church in Newport in 1698 and petitioned the governor of Massachusetts to secure a priest of the Church of England to minister to them. The governor forwarded their petition to London, where it was instrumental in the organizing of the Society for the Propagation of the Gospel in 1701.

Trinity Church, Newport, was built between 1725 and 1726. Its design resembles that of the Old North Church in Boston, an Anglican church built two years earlier and associated with the midnight ride of Paul Revere. Trinity is built with a timber frame and clapboard siding, whereas the Boston church was brick.

William Price, the designer of Old North, may have had a hand in Trinity. What is known for certain is that the builder was the talented Newport carpenter, Richard Munday. Visitors to the church are always shown not only the velvet pew where General Washington sat, but also Pew Number One, at the back, where the builder of the church had an excellent vantage point to appraise his masterpiece.

Trinity's spacious interior follows Anglican architectural traditions. The nave is longitudinal, with the entrance at one end and a curved chancel at the other.

The English Settlers: The Dissenters and the North

The English charter that gave private firms the right to settle North America divided the continent's eastern seaboard into two parts. The southern part – those lands that were to become Virginia and the Carolinas – was settled by the London Company, whose colonists were by and large staunchly loyal to the Church of England. The responsibility for colonizing the northern part – today's New England states – was given to the Plymouth Company. The pioneers who settled New England were in fundamental disagreement with many doctrines of the Anglican faith.

The Plymouth Company landed two boats full of would-be settlers at the mouth of the Kennebec River, in the present state of Maine, in August, 1607. The pioneers built a community that they called Fort St. George. They suffered through an "extreme unseasonable and frosty" winter and the next summer they abandoned the site. One of the buildings they left behind was an Anglican chapel – this first group was not made up of dissenters – which a later Spanish visitor sketched as a timber-framed structure with a gabled roof and a bell tower.

The first permanent settlers in the northern colonies were, of course, the Pilgrims. Their nucleus was a band of religious dissenters who sought the freedom to worship separately from the Church of England. When the *Mayflower* landed at Cape Cod in 1620, the Pilgrims "fell upon their knees and blessed the God of heaven, who had brought them over the vast and furious ocean, and delivered them from all the periles and miseries thereof, againe to set their feete on the firme and stable earth, their proper elemente." After a month of searching for a suitable harbour, the party of 102 men, women, and children made a final landing at Plymouth just before Christmas.

The Pilgrims had embarked on their dangerous voyage, chronicler Nathaniel Morton explains, because the "ends and aims in their Transplanting of themselves and Families, were . . . The Glory of God, the propagation of the Gospel, and the enlargement of His Majesty's Dominions." The Pilgrims called themselves Congregationalists, descendants of the Separatists, who had rejected the elaborate ritual and authoritarian clergy of the Church of England. Their religious beliefs, influenced by Calvinism, demanded a return to the simpler service of primitive Christianity. Their social beliefs were democratic; civil government, like church government, rested in the hands of each individual member of the congregation – hence the name Congregationalist.

To the Pilgrims, church government and civil authority were the reverse sides of the same coin; one result of this close association was that when the Pilgrims built their houses of worship, the structures were never intended as churches only. Religious meetings were held in what they called meeting houses – buildings that might today be labelled "multi-purpose assembly buildings." For several years the Plymouth brethren worshipped on the ground floor of the colony's sturdy fort. Above them, as they prayed, six iron cannon stood in readiness.

Ten years after the Pilgrims had established the Plymouth colony, another group of dissenters under John Winthrop established the Massachusetts Bay colony. In the 1630s some 20,000 newcomers, escaping from the religious persecution of Charles I, arrived at the site of present-day Boston to join Winthrop's initial group. These settlers were Puritans: Congregationalists like the Plymouth group, but more militantly opposed to church tradition and less tolerant of those who disagreed with their reforms. Their name came from their intent to "purify" the Church of England. The Puritan Church became the state religion of the colony and citizenship was granted only to members. Non-believers could face the death penalty.

Capitalizing on a loophole in the company's royal charter, the Puritans placed their seat of government in the New World. This fact speeded the growth of the colony and assured its success. Within a decade the Puritans had established numerous new town-sites. Freed from the restrictions that hampered other colonies, Massachusetts' settlers developed methods and laws that suited their particular situation. They developed diversified agriculture, which gave farmers a degree of self-sufficiency. This, combined with the religious authorities' desire to maintain a close spiritual hold on their adherents, led to the development of rows of small towns, each centred around a village green, at the side of which was situated the meeting house. Homes were built nearby. When a town grew so large that people had to travel a great distance to reach the meeting house, a new town would be established. In 1635 the General Court, or legislature, of Massachusetts decreed that "hereafter noe dwelling house shall be builte above half a myle from the meeting house." (The letter of the law was unenforceable and it was repealed five years later.) Farm plots further from the village centre were apportioned among the residents.

The Puritans' meeting house, like the Pilgrims', was the centre of both religious and temporal government. "Places intended for the sacred worship of God," wrote clergyman and author Cotton Mather, "may lawfully be put into any civil service for which they may be accommodated at the times when the sacred worship is not there to be attended." Simplicity was the architectural keynote. "The setting of these places off with a theatrical gaudiness," he continued, "does not savor of the spirit of a true Christian society." And a meeting house should

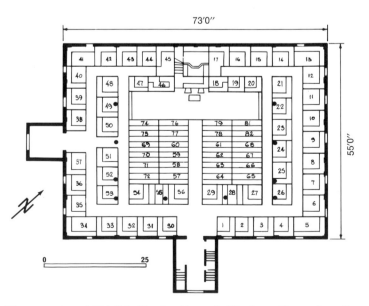

The floor plan of Old Ship Meeting House in Hingham, Massachusetts.

never be called a "church." Mather's grandfather, Richard, who had come over as a minister in 1635, insisted that "there is no just ground from the Scriptures to apply such a trope as church to a house for a public assembly."

The architecture of the meeting house reflects its dual role as a place for both religious and civil assembly, and represents the rejection of the worldly ostentation of the traditional church. In Europe the Pilgrims and the Puritans had been persecuted for their beliefs, and the practice of their religion had been secretive. Usually they had met in private houses or, when permitted by law, in existing parish churches. The pioneers accordingly produced a synthesis of the religious and secular buildings they had used in England, a synthesis uniquely appropriate to New England circumstances.

The only seventeenth-century meeting house to survive until our day is the renowned Old Ship Meeting House in Hingham, Massachusetts, begun in 1681. Through the years the structure was altered; its present aspect – the result of a 1930 restoration – is closest to its mid-eighteenth-century form.

In 1680 the residents of Hingham agreed to "build a new meeting house with all convenient speed," and records show that they discussed its dimensions but not its form; like the parishioners of St. Peter's in Virginia, they took that for granted. The builder was Charles Stockbridge, an owner and builder of mills from nearby Scituate. The two principal carpenters were Steven and Joshua Lincoln of Hingham. To finance the building, every taxpayer was assessed according to his wealth.

The Old Ship Meeting House is nearly square, with its principal entrance on one of the longer sides. Two storeys of rectangular windows punctuate the walls. Above them the hip roof tapers from each side; instead of meeting at a point, it ends in a rectangular "captain's walk," which is surrounded by a railing and surmounted by a belfry. The simple, chunky rectangular shape reflects the Congregational ideal of a return to the severe simplicity of primitive Christianity.

The interior is equally austere. Its most conspicuous feature is the tall pulpit, located in the centre of the long wall opposite the entrance. Each pew faces the pulpit, as do the galleries that project from the other three walls. The pews immediately in front of the pulpit are reserved for the deacons and the elders of the congregation, and before them stands a small communion table. There are no crosses, no paintings, no sculpture, no screens, no chancel – nothing. Over the congregation rise massive roof timbers that were discovered during restoration after having spent two centuries concealed behind a ceiling. The resemblance of the unusual curved struts to an overturned ship's hull gives the meeting house its name.

As originally built in 1681 the Old Ship Meeting House was considerably smaller than it is today. Its roof was steeper and supported a small belfry. The main entrance and the pulpit faced each other on the long walls, not the same walls they occupy today.

Although the New England settlers could look to England for no precise architectural form on which to model their meeting houses, they creatively combined two familiar prototypes. First, from the English parish church they took the idea of a rectangular hall with the pulpit on one long side opposite a door. In effect, the Anglican church was rotated ninety degrees and its chancel door became the principal entrance. Second, they borrowed from the market halls and town halls of England many of the external features that distinguish the Old Ship Meeting House – the hip roof, the balustraded platform,

the crowning turret. The new form produced by this amalgamation was dictated in part by the materials the colonists had to work with and by the talents they could muster.

The buildings were constructed of solid timber frame covered with clapboards, the most common method in New England. The wedge-shaped boards were split or "riven" from logs and nailed to the frame so that each row of clapboards covered the exposed upper edge of the row below. It was an excellent system for warding off the driving snow and rain of the harsh coastal winters. Clapboard construction had been used in southeastern England, particularly for farm buildings, but was not widespread there in the seventeenth century. The settlers quickly realized its value in their new environment. Brick was not popular because there was no ready supply of lime for mortar.

The earliest meeting house whose appearance was recorded is the meeting house built in 1638 at Dedham, Massachusetts. It is a timber-framed building thirty feet by twenty feet in size and twelve feet high, with a gabled roof. The simple structure reflects the same sources as the Old Ship Meeting House, but in a more primitive form: gables are found frequently in English market halls and the elongated rectangular shape is close to the proportions of a parish church. Meeting houses up and down the New England coast perpetuated this style well into the eighteenth century.

One of the most beautiful of early meeting houses is at Sandown, New Hampshire. Erected in 1773-1774, its workmanship, possibly by Sandown carpenter Peter Colby, is marvellously high in quality. The pristine building is nearly square, and can be entered on three sides. The two pilasters which frame each entrance, and the triangular pediments that they support, are carved with delicate Georgian detail. The cornice below the eaves is equally exquisite.

The fine exterior proportions are complemented by those of the interior. A ceiling – probably original – hides the roof timbers. Only the knee braces beneath the tie beams are exposed. The original furnishings remain, with their hardware intact. In the centre of the north wall is a fine wineglass pulpit of stained pine, so named because of its goblet-like shape. The minister stands silhouetted against an arched window and framed by marbled columns. A delicately spindled staircase

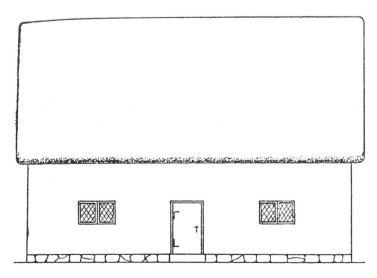

First Meeting House, Dedham, Massachusetts (Donnelly: *The New England Meeting Houses of the Seventeenth Century*, 1968).

The tower of West Parish Meeting House at West Barnstable, Cape Cod.

One band of New Englanders explored the Saint John River valley. They decided that this region on the west shore of the Bay of Fundy would make an excellent base for trading with New England ports and with local Indians, as well as for farming. A large group of settlers from Essex County in Massachusetts moved in 1763 to the new township of Maugerville (pronounced "majorville"), the first community to be established on the Saint John River. It had been named after Joshua Mauger, a Halifax merchant who helped the settlers acquire the land.

The congregation was organized soon after settlement. At first, meetings were held in private homes; construction of the meeting house began in 1775. The building followed the traditional New England form, with the addition of a western tower, which gives the buildings a distinct longitudinal axis. The structure was claimed to be a replica of the Congregational meeting house at Rowley, Massachusetts, which had been home to many of the Maugerville settlers.

When the Declaration of Independence was proclaimed in 1776, Maugerville's citizens resolved "to submit ourselves to the government of Massachusetts Bay." The Congregationalists of Maugerville suddenly found themselves surrounded by hostile Loyalist neighbours who resented their open support of the revolution. The situation was tense and open violence seemed inevitable. In a move that required a large amount of imagination laced with a massive infusion of tact, the Congregationalists decided to transport their meeting house, the most visible symbol of discord, to a new site at nearby Sheffield. In December, 1788, workers began the intricate and tedious task of lifting the building off its foundation with screw jacks. In the following March a hundred oxen hauled the meeting house five miles down the river road to Sheffield. It arrived undamaged; the only work needed at the destination was a new foundation and some carpentry repairs to the steeple.

raises him to a level where he is as visible and audible to worshippers in the gallery as he is to those below. The large sounding board above his head helps to project his voice. Beneath the pulpit sits the deacon's pew, and a drop-leaf shelf hinged against the front of the pew serves as a communion table.

Not all builders of meeting houses continued the Puritan tradition unchanged. Rival Anglicans had begun building churches in New England, buildings almost always more monumental and more ornate than the simple Puritan meeting houses. The Puritans could not help but be impressed. As a result, by the beginning of the eighteenth century, bell towers began to appear at the ends of meeting houses. The Puritans' altering perceptions about their place of worship demanded a share of the monumentality that distinguished the Anglican churches. This new influence appears, for example, in the West Parish Meeting House at West Barnstable, Massachusetts.

New England's population increased and colonists began to search for suitable new lands, but the British government discouraged settlement in the Indian lands to the west and instead offered New Englanders an alternative. In 1755 the government expelled the Acadian French from their homeland in Nova Scotia. Governor Charles Lawrence of Nova Scotia offered the farmland vacated by the Acadians – land "cultivated for more than a hundred years past"– free to all Protestants. Even though the Church of England became the established denomination, Lawrence proclaimed that "Protestant dissenters from the Church of England, whether they be Calvinists, Lutherans, Quakers or under what denomination whatsoever, shall have free liberty of conscience and may erect and build meeting houses for public worship."

This meeting house at Sheffield, New Brunswick, travelled from Maugerville in 1789.

After two centuries of development as a unique response to the need for a home for religious and temporal government, the colonial meeting house came to an end around the year 1800. Many old meeting houses were the victims of "churchification": the addition of a tower and other trappings, for example, at Old Covenanters' Meeting House in Horton, Nova Scotia. Throughout New England – as in the Maritimes – Congregationalists began to erect houses of worship that were longitudinal in plan and had towers or steeples, and they even started to call them "churches." The first Congregational Church in Milford, Connecticut, built in 1823, demonstrates this last stage in this reversion to English parish church forms.

In its heyday, however, the Puritan meeting house exerted an influence on its neighbours in much the same way that it had been influenced by Anglican forms. In 1707 the Anglican parishioners of St. Paul's in Kingston (also called Narragansett), Rhode Island, built a church that frankly displays its source of inspiration. It has the familiar meeting house façade, two storeys high and five windows wide, with the door in the centre of one long wall. Only the traditionally Anglican arched windows and the ornate pedimented doorway betray the congregation's distaste for Puritan plainness.

Anglicans had originally been denied citizenship in New England; not until 1688 were they permitted public worship. They were censured again before the revolution for their generally pro-royalist politics, and in 1774, on the eve of the Revolutionary War, St. Paul's was closed. In 1799 it was moved five miles north to the friendlier town of Wickford, where it rests today.

Rhode Island's first Anglican parish had been Trinity in the city of Newport. (St. Paul's in Kingston was the second.) A number of parishioners in Newport were Huguenots who had fled from France when the edict protecting them from persecution was revoked. With the help of the Society for the Propaga-

This lovely oval window graces Trinity Church at Newport, Rhode Island.

tion of the Gospel in Foreign Parts, the parish built its first church in 1702. The impressive Trinity Church of today dates from 1725-1726.

Trinity is one of the largest of eighteenth-century New England churches. Its rectangular body has two tiers of arched windows. The tall tower is surmounted by arched stages terminating in a spire, which stretches some 150 feet above the ground. The tower may be an addition of about 1762. At that time the nave was extended by thirty feet by sawing the church in half and inserting two extra bays.

The Society for the Propagation of the Gospel also propagated a particular kind of church in which the faith was to be celebrated – the three-aisled basilica, which originated with the churches of the earliest Christians and which survived as the basis of the newest parish churches in London. At Trinity builder Richard Munday, a talented Newport carpenter, translated this British source into a building that is wholly of New England in its loving use of wood, inside and out. His design was influenced by the Puritan meeting house: it incorporates secular-looking, shuttered, two-storeyed exterior walls and a prominently placed central pulpit.

In Nova Scotia the Church of England arrived with the first English settlers in 1749. St. Paul's church in Halifax was the earliest church of that denomination in Nova Scotia. Its design was based on that of Gibbs' Marybone Chapel in London (now known as St. Peter's, Vere Street). Many parish churches in the countryside, such as St. Mary's at Auburn, followed its imposing British example architecturally.

More intimate is the church of St. Edward's at nearby Clementsport, built in 1795. The frame structure provides an

St. Paul's Anglican Church, Kingston, Rhode Island, looks like a meeting house.

St. Thomas' Anglican Church, St. John's, Newfoundland, known as the Old Garrison Church for its service to the British Military.

attractive compromise between the traditions of meeting house and church. Its longitudinal plan, with a spire over the western door and a projecting chancel, reveals its Anglican leanings. The side, in contrast, has a five-window elevation with a central doorway characteristic of the meeting house. The pedimented south doorway has simplified classical elements, enjoying the delicacy and finesse so typical of the best Maritime wood-carving.

By about 1800 the church and the meeting house were losing their identities as distinct building types. After two centuries of settlement along the east coast, the sharp lines originally drawn between Anglicans and dissenters had been blurred in architecture and society alike. This cultural diffusion in New England and the Maritime provinces of Canada created a tradition of fine wood construction that profoundly influenced the builders of churches across the continent.

The Settlement of the Middle Colonies

Around the turn of the seventeenth century, English navigator Henry Hudson was hired by the Dutch East India Company for $320 – and the promise to pay his wife eighty dollars more should he never return – to find a passage to the Orient by way of the Russian Arctic. Instead, Hudson and his mixed crew of Dutch and English sailors made their landfall at Newfoundland, skirted Cape Cod, and sighted the Virginia Coast. From there they turned northward, noted the mouth of the Delaware River, entered the bay of New York, and sailed up the river that bears his name, as far as the present-day site of Albany. When Hudson determined that the narrowing river did not lead to China, he claimed the territory for Holland and went home.

The following year a small Dutch expedition bartered very lucratively with the Indians: Holland had entered the fur trade. Settlement of the province of New Netherland began in earnest in 1624 under the direction of the newly organized Dutch West India Company. Director Peter Minuit entered his famous negotiations with the Indians and purchased Manhattan, naming it Fort Amsterdam, later New Amsterdam, the capital of the colony. Other Dutch settlers made their homes along the banks of the Hudson River under the sponsorship of *patroons*, who for their efforts received power similar to those of feudal lords.

The Dutch West India Company sent along ministers of the Dutch Reformed Church. Despite grandiose plans to build fine churches in the new capital, the first house of worship was a very makeshift thing. A settler reported in 1626 that the local millwright was "busy building a horse mill over which shall be constructed a spacious room sufficient to accommodate a large congregation." An intended belfry was never installed.

Sixteen years later the colony still had no proper church. Captain David Pietersen de Vries, a *patroon* who wrote an account of his life in America, related how he bullied Director Willem Kieft into building a fitting house of worship. De Vries complained that when the English visited they saw only a mean barn for public worship. "In English settlements the first thing they do is build a church, and you don't have any decent church here. You're a good churchman, why don't you build a church?"

When the burghers were in the local tavern celebrating the marriage of the stepdaughter of the Reverend Everardus Bogardus, the resourceful director started a public subscription for a new church. "The Director," reported de Vries, "set off to work after the fourth or fifth drink; and he himself setting a liberal example, let the wedding guests sign whatever they were disposed to give towards the church. Each, then, with a light head, subscribed away at a handsome rate, one competing with the other; and although some heartily repented it when their senses came back, they were obliged nevertheless to pay."

Thus well endowed, and with a little help from company funds, the church was begun. Two Englishmen named Ogden, from Stamford in what is now Connecticut, were the builders. The building was seventy-two feet by fifty-two feet and had walls of stone covered by oak shingles. A pair of gables, one of them surmounted by a belfry, faced the street.

The broad rectangle was only one of several types of plan being used in Holland for Dutch Reformed churches. Other architects experimented with the octagonal plan, a shape felt to be particularly appropriate to the Calvinist emphasis on preaching. In 1641 *patroon* Kiliaen Van Rensselaer sent to the overseer of his American manor near Albany "a wooden model of a small church . . . the shape being mostly that of an eight-cornered mill." Whether or not the church built at Rensselaerwyck was octagonal is uncertain, but octagonal churches were erected in the years that followed at Brooklyn, Bushwick, Jamaica, and New Utrecht on Long Island, and in Bergen, Hackensack, and the Ponds in New Jersey. None has survived, but an illustration of the church at Bergen (by a builder named Willem Day) shows it to have been small and capped with a very steep roof.

In their search for a prototype for the houses of worship for their new religion, the early Dutch builders apparently looked to mills – perhaps their most important secular public buildings – just as the New England Puritans had set upon the

Dutch Reformed Church in Bergen, New Jersey (Winfield: *History of the County of Hudson*, 1874).

English town hall. As time passed, the Dutch builders settled on the more conventional four-sided churches, perhaps because rectangular buildings were easier to erect than octagonal ones. The Dutch Reformed church built in Albany in 1715 was rectangular, with its steep, hipped roof topped by a cupola. In many respects it resembled the houses of worship built by another Calvinist group – the New England Congregationalists, who also came to America by way of Holland, and with whom the Dutch communicated on American soil.

New Netherland was taken over by England in 1664 and New Amsterdam became New York; but in upstate New York, the Dutch settlers maintained their language and their faith long after they lost their independence. Churches, too, continued to be built in the traditional way. The Fort Herkimer Reformed Dutch Church in the Mohawk River valley, built by a congregation dominated by newly arrived Germans who were also of the Reformed faith, was begun in 1730. When hostilities broke out with the French and Indians, the half-built stone structure was quickly roofed in and pressed into service as an auxiliary defence to nearby Fort Herkimer. In 1812 the height of the building was increased some eight feet, a balcony and second row of windows added, and the entrance shifted from the north side to the west end.

Shortly after the Dutch had established themselves at New Amsterdam, the first Swedish expedition arrived at the mouth of the Delaware River under the command of none other than Peter Minuit, the former director of the New Netherland colony, now in Swedish service. The adventurers built Fort Christina – named after the Swedish queen – on the site of Wilmington, Delaware, and called their territory New Sweden. Neither the English nor the Dutch appreciated the new competition. In 1655 the Dutch defeated the Swedes in bloodless battle and New Sweden came to an end after only seventeen years, although her settlers remained.

The first Swedish churches were built of wood, presumably of round logs laid horizontally. It was the Swedes who intro-

Dutch Reformed Church, Herkimer County, shows signs of renovation.

Dutch Reformed Church in Albany, New York (Egbert: "Religious Expression in American Architecture," 1961).

duced log cabin construction to America, and not the English or the natives. German settlers likewise brought log construction over from the Old World. Before long, this way of building would become the standard manner on the frontier. A new mythology would, in time, transform the log cabin into a precious symbol of American democracy.

In 1697, three young Lutheran missionaries left Sweden to serve the small Swedish-American community. Two of them promptly directed construction of new masonry parish churches. One of the newcomers was the twenty-nine-year-old Reverend Eric Björk, formerly a tutor in the home of one of King Charles xi's most trusted advisors, who harangued the congregation at Fort Christina into replacing its old log church.

The builders of the new house of worship were all Englishmen from Philadelphia, presumably chosen because no skilled Swedes could be found to do the job. A contract entered into with mason Joseph Yard stipulated that he and his three sons should "lay all the stone and Brick work . . . from ye foundation to the lower ends of the windows 3 foot thick, and then afterwards 2 foot thick upwards, and all ye Windows and doors upon the Church shall be Arched, and the doors and Windows Arched and Quined [quoined] with Bricks." Granite was collected from nearby farms and broken on the site. Pastor Björk and churchwarden Charles Springer went from door to door seeking day labourers.

Old Swedes Church, Wilmington, Delaware, required arched stone porches to stop the spreading of its walls. In 1802 the tower and belfry were added.

As originally built, Old Swedes (consecrated in 1699 as *Helga Trefaldighet Kyrcka* – "Holy Trinity Church") was a simple rectangle measuring thirty-six feet by sixty-six feet. The congregation gave the builders specifications of a general nature only; they worked out the details in the manner to which they were accustomed. The church has a Scandinavian flavour presumably because of Björk's constant presence by the sides of his builders. When the question arose, for example, as to how the gable ends should be treated, the carpenters argued for full gables, whereas the original intention had apparently been for a lower and more economical hipped roof. A compromise was reached by building the gables only halfway up, and the present "jerkin-headed" or "gambrel" roof resulted. (It survives only at the east end.) The result looks more like the kind of church building to which the Swede Björk was accustomed. Once again, the pioneers reconciled the ideal prototype with the practicalities of the new situation. However, the compromise was costly: the walls began to spread shortly after the church was finished.

Gloria Dei Church in Philadelphia, also known as Old Swedes, was built at the same time to serve the oldest congregation of any denomination in Philadelphia. Its pastor, Reverend Andrew Rudman, had come to America with Björk. The same tradesmen who had built the Wilmington church returned to Philadelphia and finished the new building in 1700. The

builders repeated their structural mistakes and the walls of the simple brick rectangular structure immediately began to spread under the weight of the roof. In 1704 a sacristy was placed against one side as a buttress, and a vestibule along the other. The tower was added some time later. The roof is steeper than those on English churches and the polygonal sanctuary was wholly new to the American colonies. Both are features remembered from Swedish church design. The will of the Swedish congregation and the skill of the English builder again combined to produce a unique compromise.

The largest contingent of Lutherans to emigrate to America were Germans, who first trickled into the American colonies in the seventeenth century. After 1700 thousands more bought up much of the cheap, rich farmland of Pennsylvania. The settlers built their houses of logs, much as they had back home. These newcomers became known as Pennsylvania *Deutsch* – a term today corrupted into Pennsylvania Dutch.

Augustus Lutheran Church in Trappe, Pennsylvania, was probably built to the specifications of its first preacher, Reverend Henry Melchoir Muhlenberg, founder of the first Lutheran synod in North America. The church offers a fine expression of Muhlenberg's religious beliefs and ethnic roots. Lutheran worship is liturgical, placing great importance upon the Eucharist; hence the plan is longitudinal, with the main entrance at one end and the sanctuary, reserved for communion, at the other.

The Lutherans also share the Protestant emphasis on the spoken word; therefore the panelled walnut pulpit is raised high along a side wall and surrounded by balconies to allow more people to get closer to the minister. The German architectural heritage shows through clearly in the polygonal sanctuary and in the double-sloped gambrel roof.

In contrast to the Lutherans – who quickly assimilated to American life and spoke, dressed, and worked as their neighbours – stand the "Plain People," those German-speaking immigrants who dressed plainly, lived simply, and kept unto themselves. These were the Mennonites, the Amish, and the Dunkers (or Dunkards). Their strict adherence to the teachings of the New Testament, their refusal to hold public office, and their determined pacifism led many to live only among their own people, shut off from the outside world. Strictest, perhaps, are the Amish, named after Jacob Amman, a Swiss Mennonite bishop of the seventeenth century. They oppose the use of church buildings, and worship in barns or dwellings instead.

Escaping European persecution, thirteen Mennonite families settled in what came to be known as Germantown, Pennsylvania (now a suburb of Philadelphia), in 1683. Many more followed over the years. The Germantown congregation built the first Mennonite meeting house in America a few years later. Their present meeting house, rebuilt in 1770, retains many of the original features. It is a plan building of stone, containing a single room. The austere design makes it indistinguishable from a house.

More isolationist even than the Mennonites were the Seventh Day Baptists or Seventh Day Dunkers. ("Dunker" derives from the German word *tunken*, "to immerse," and refers to the group's baptism by immersion.) The sect was organized by Johann Konrad Beissel, a Palatinate German who established a monastic religious community called the Cloister at Ephrata, Pennsylvania. The believers, numbering 300 members at the peak, owned all goods in common and were economically self-sufficient. Most practised celibacy, which severely retarded the growth of their numbers. The two surviving buildings of the Cloister were erected in the 1740s: the *Saal* was the house of worship and common hall; women lived in the *Saron*, or "Sister House." The *Bethania*, or "Brother House," was demolished early in this country.

The wall of the *Saal* are framed with hewn oak timbers filled with stones and clay, and protected with oak clapboards. The roofs are covered by shakes that are lapped on the sides as well as top and bottom – a manner said to be common in parts of the Rhine Valley and Bavaria. Within the large principal room are plain benches and a table for worship. The *Saron* is built of hewn oak logs, making it a kind of gigantic log cabin. Poplar clapboards once protected the logs from the weather. Inside, winding staircases and long, narrow passageways lead to tiny cells.

Another German-speaking pietistic group were the Moravians, a pacifistic, but not isolationist, sect. In the Oley Valley near Reading, Pennsylvania, a Moravian community built a meeting house of half-timbered construction, their customary method. Familiar in Europe and once popular in America, this mode of construction has now become almost extinct. The spaces between the timbers are filled with brick and covered

with plaster. (The *Saal* at Ephrata was built similarly, but covered with clapboards.)

These German sects chose Pennsylvania as their home because of the religious liberty promised in that colony's charter from Charles II to founder William Penn of the Society of Friends, better known as Quakers. The Friends insisted that all persons were equal in the eyes of God, and therefore held to the ministry of all believers. Because they had no ministers or liturgy, they laid out their meeting houses without pulpits or altars. This pattern was followed at Old Kennett Friends' Meeting House, built of stone in 1710 in a community thirty miles west of Philadelphia. Most Friends' meeting houses have two entrance doors along the long side. Women enter through one door and men by the other. A partition separates the auditorium into two parts for business meetings, and is removed at meetings for worship.

Both Quaker and Mennonite meeting houses look very much like private homes, characteristic of the meeting houses of so-called left-wing Protestant denominations. They are decidedly humbler and plainer than those of the Congregationalists and the Dutch Reformed. The Congregationalists stripped the English parish church of many of its architectural trappings and combined it with the architectural tradition of the town hall. The Friends, on the other hand, began with the house and enlarged or extended it where necessary. Like many of the new radical Protestant groups, they had begun in Europe by worshipping covertly in private houses; moreover, they felt that they were returning to the practices of the earliest Christians, who likewise prayed in homes. Even though their appearances may at times be similar, the two kinds of meeting houses had different historical beginnings.

The magnificent meeting house built by the Shakers in New Lebanon, New York, is three storeys high in front (and four at the gabled ends), but despite its size and scale it remains decidedly domestic in appearance. An offshoot of the Friends, the Shakers came to America in 1774 and began this, their first meeting house, in 1785. Their members were officially called the "United Society of Believers in Christ's Second Appearing," but were first labelled the "Shaking Quakers."

The Baptists and the Presbyterians, like the Friends, erected house-type meeting houses. American Baptists trace their origins to Roger Williams, a Puritan teacher who was banished from the Massachusetts Bay Colony for having espoused religious liberty. He settled on a site south of the Plymouth Colony that he called Providence. Under Williams' direction Rhode Island developed as a colony that, in his words, "might be for a shelter for persons distressed for conscience."

The plain and cubic Elder Ballou Meeting House, near Providence, was built around 1740 by the Six Principle Baptist Church. The Ballou family were among the first to settle this Rhode Island district early in the eighteenth century. The meeting house is named after Abner Ballou, an elder of the society who served from 1775 until his death in 1806.

Born out of the teachings of John Calvin, Presbyterianism grew quickly in America after 1700 with the emigration of the Ulster Scots, or Scotch-Irish. Many of them disembarked at Philadelphia or at New Castle, a short distance below Wilmington on the Delaware River. When the Scottish Reverend John Wilson arrived at New Castle in 1698, the local Dutch Reformed congregation invited him to become their pastor. The church joined the Presbyterian fold, boasting a congregation composed of Dutch, Huguenots, Scots, and Calvinist English. As more Presbyterians arrived and settled inland,

Old Swedes Church, Philadelphia, built by members of one of the many Christian denominations that settled in Pennsylvania.

Top: The interior of New Castle Presbyterian Church, Delaware. Bottom: the exterior.

the New Castle church became a kind of mother church to the newer congregations. The red brick New Castle Presbyterian Church was built in 1707 and enlarged five years later. Originally a single arched window lay on either side of a central doorway. The two-bay extension and a later vestibule shifted the principal entrance from a long side to a short end – a pattern which recurred time and again as meeting houses were metamorphosed into churches.

The American colonies also became home to a number of European Jews. The immigrants were all Sephardim, descendants of the Jews who had been expelled from Spain and Portugal at the end of the fifteenth century. A small Jewish community in Newport, Rhode Island, decided to build a synagogue after a century of worshipping in private homes. As architect they chose Peter Harrison, a former sea captain and shipowner of Newport who had trained himself to become the most accomplished designer in colonial New England. Sod was broken for Congregation Jeshuat Israel in 1759. The twenty or so Jewish families in Newport gave what money they could towards its building, and contributions came in from London, Amsterdam, New York, and the Caribbean. The lovely little building was opened on December 2, 1763, during the feast of Hanukkah.

Americans had little idea of what a synagogue really should look like; the only synagogue in the colonies was one in New York. Harrison was instructed in the building's liturgical needs by Dr. Isaac de Abraham Touro, the congregation's rabbi, who was newly arrived from the Rabbinical Academy in Amsterdam. To the delight of congregation and townsfolk alike, Harrison created a gem of a building, with a brick exterior enlivened by two tiers of delicate arched windows, a graceful classical porch, a modillion cornice at the top, and a low hipped roof. A discreet two-storey extension at the left contains school rooms as well as a staircase for access to the balcony.

The interior follows Sephardic tradition by placing the reader's desk near the centre, and the ark for the Torah scrolls against the eastern wall. (The eastern European Jews, called Ashkenazim, place the reader's desk at the east end next to the ark.) The men sit on the ground floor, with the officers of the synagogue on raised seats against the north side. The women, as is customary, occupy the balcony.

In the Touro Synagogue, as in his other designs, Harrison showed a dedication to the classical compositions of recent English architects. His was the method typical of the Georgian architects of the eighteenth century. His professionalism is indicative of the fact that America had grown from a society of pioneers to one of sophisticated city dwellers. No longer did buildings result from imprecise memories of the traditional architecture in the settlers' overseas homeland, passed on to craftsmen who worked according to folk custom. Now, because of the proliferation of books and learning, the urbanity of taste, and the specialization of trades, the lay builder had been supplanted by the professional architect who studied and emulated the latest architectural developments in Europe.

Touro Synagogue in Newport was dedicated in 1763.

LUTHERANS AND PLAIN PEOPLE IN PENNSYLVANIA

The Germans who immigrated to America after 1700 were primarily from the western German province of the Rhenish Palatinate. Wars and crop failures forced them to leave their homes and flee to England; from there they were sent to New York and finally settled in Pennsylvania. The majority of the "Pennsylvania Dutch" [Deutsch] were Lutheran. Their first churches were small and poor. But in 1742, the dedicated young Reverend Henry Melchior Muhlenberg arrived in America and began to organize all of the Lutheran congregations from New York to Maryland. Muhlenberg's own church, Augustus Lutheran (above), was named after Herman Augustus Francke, the founder of the Halle Institutions.

Lutherans were quickly and easily assimilated into the mainstream of American society. But there were German nonconformist sects among the Pennsylvania pioneers — including Mennonites, Amish, and Dunkers — who chose to live differently and separately. The first Mennonites in Pennsylvania, who arrived in 1683, built the austere meeting house shown on the opposite page.

Above and right: Augustus Lutheran Church in Trappe, Pennsylvania.
Opposite: a Mennonite meeting house at Germantown, Pennsylvania.

SHAKERS IN NEW YORK, QUAKERS IN MARYLAND

William Penn proposed to the King of England, Charles II, a settlement in the woods of America to be called "Sylvania." Charles insisted on improving the name by adding a prefix in honour of Penn's father.

Penn arrived at the mouth of the Delaware River in 1682 with a cargo of smallpox-ridden colonists. A settlement dedicated to religious toleration was laid out, beginning with the "City of Brotherly Love," Philadelphia.

A sect that came to be known as the Shakers was an offshoot of the Society of Friends. The name comes from their practice of marching around the ground floors of meeting houses, wrestling with evil and the promptings of the devil by using shaking or gyrating movements. The Shakers came to America in 1774 and began their first meeting house in New Lebanon, New York (opposite), in 1785.

The oldest Quaker meeting house in America is not in Philadelphia, but in Easton, Maryland (above and right), where the Third Haven Meeting House still stands. Friends assembled here twenty-five years before Penn's arrival, and the English Quaker, George Fox, visited the area in 1672. The present meeting house was built around 1684 and enlarged a century later.

Opposite: the original Shaker Meeting House at New Lebanon, New York, was built in 1785. The Shakers, or Shaking Quakers, were an offshoot of the Society of Friends, whose Third Haven Meeting House at Easton, Maryland (above and right), is the oldest Quaker meeting house in America.

GREENOCK PRESBYTERIAN, ST. ANDREWS, NEW BRUNSWICK

Presbyterianism established its firmest roots in the Scotland of John Knox. Knox began his ministry in 1547 and, after meeting Calvin at Geneva in 1554, brought many of his ideas back to Britain. Knox initiated Scottish Presbyterianism's emphasis on the necessity of a rigorous education for all. He advocated a national system of schooling to include a school in every parish. Many Scots immigrated to Canada and the United States during the eighteenth and nineteenth centuries, bringing their Presbyterianism with them. Canada's first schools and the United States' first universities developed largely because of their tradition.

The Scots who came to New Brunswick cultivated root crops and exploited the commercial advantages of their proximity to the sea. One of their immediate aims was to build churches in which they could continue their religious practices. The church at St. Andrews (on the opposite page) was originally contracted in 1821 but, because funds ran out, a local

citizen, Captain Christopher Scott, took the initiative and had the building completed three years later. Scott accepted the privilege of naming the church, which still bears the name of his Scottish birthplace.

While the simplicity of the church's design makes it appropriate to Presbyterian worship, there are decorative and practical additions, like the subtle classical trim under the eaves, the front entrance, and the Wren-like spire. The green oak design underneath the clock on the spire was meant by Scott as a play of words on the church's name. The medallion embossed in plaster, which decorates the ceiling, and the impressive two-tiered pulpit at the east end provide Greenock's interior with a simple but attractive dignity.

Above: Ye Olde Yellow Meeting House, Imlaystown, New Jersey, is a simple rural Baptist church built in 1737. It has two storeys, a double entrance, and is covered with wooden clapboard. Opposite: the exterior of Greenock Presbyterian, St. Andrews, New Brunswick (top), is also a rectangular, two-storeyed structure; the interior (bottom, right) is simply finished, and the elegant steeple (bottom, left) has the date of the church's completion on it.

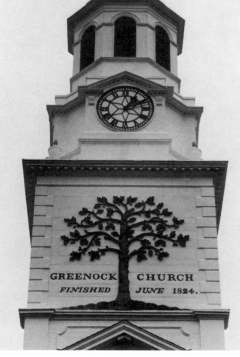

TWO INDIAN CHURCHES

The Indian Castle Church in Herkimer County, New York, near the small community of Little Falls (above), was built for the Mohawk Indians in 1769-1770. Sir William Johnson, Superintendent of Indians, paid for the structure out of his own pocket in an effort to ensure the natives' loyalty to the British cause. Loyal they remained, and during the Revolutionary War the Indians fought for Britain and then immigrated to Canada. In the years that followed, various congregations inherited the vacated church, each making its own alterations in the original building. In 1855 a Union Church Society moved it a few yards and altered it to conform to the new Greek Revival taste.

Her Majesty's Chapel of the Mohawks (St. Paul's), Brantford, Ontario (opposite), is the only Indian chapel that has been royally dedicated. The great Mohawk chief, Joseph Brant, who had been educated at the expense of Sir William Johnson and who had lived for a while near the Indian Castle Church, led the Iroquois against the Americans during the revolution. After the war he and his followers fled to southern Ontario, where they were given a huge tract of land along the Grand River. At Brantford, named after the Indian Loyalist leader, the British government built the natives a wooden Anglican chapel dedicated to St. Paul. George III donated a set of Royal Arms. Her Majesty's Chapel of the Mohawks, as it is known today, has been altered since its erection in 1785. The church remains one of the few royal chapels in Canada.

Above: the Indian Castle Church in Herkimer County, New York, was built by the British to ensure the loyalty of the local Indians to the British forces during the American Revolutionary War. Opposite: the church that the British built for the Indians in Brantford, Ontario, to thank them for their loyalty back in New York state during the war. It is called Her Majesty's Chapel of the Mohawks, or St. Paul's.

THE "DUTCH" IN NORTH AMERICA

Not far behind Peter Minuit and the West India Company's traders and settlers came the dedicated ministers of the Dutch Reformed Church. The Dutch involvement in North America began with a letter from Captain John Smith to the English navigator Henry Hudson, who was then in the employ of the Dutch East India Company. Smith's description of the Virginia coastline promised that there was "a sea leading into the Western ocean by the north of the southern English colony." Hudson's journey in 1609 up the river that bears his name is a familiar story.

The first Dutch church in North America in Fort (later New) Amsterdam was a room above a mill. The more fitting churches that followed alternated at first between peculiarly Dutch octagons and more mundane rectangles. The latter won out, probably because of the example set by rectangular English

churches. The Dutch Reformed congregation at Red Hook, New York, midway up the Hudson River, built such a church (above) in the 1750s.

The Old Dutch Church in Halifax, Nova Scotia (opposite), is not really Dutch at all. It was founded by a group of German Lutheran immigrants who exchanged some lumber for a small house and then dragged it to its site "by the united effort of voluntary hands in the year 1756." During the next four years they enlarged it and added a steeple.

Above: the Old Red Church at Red Hook, New York, blends sturdy building traditions with a sense of graceful form. Opposite: the Old Dutch (actually German) Church, as old St. George's Church is called, Halifax, Nova Scotia. It was converted to a church from a dwelling that had been constructed a few years earlier. Both churches were built in the 1750s.

THE CLOISTER, EPHRATA, PENNSYLVANIA

Two buildings dating from the 1740s (on the previous two pages) are all that remain of a monastic religious sect known variously as the Seventh Day Baptists, the Seventh Day Dunkers, or the Society of the Solitary. They established a community called the Cloister at Ephrata, Pennsylvania, some sixty miles west of Philadelphia. At its peak the group numbered three hundred believers. The remaining buildings — abandoned in the 1920s — are the house of worship and common hall of the group, called the *Saal,* and the *Saron,* or Sister House, where the women lived. The *Bethania,* or Brother House, was demolished a half-century ago.

A visitor to the Cloister might think that he had been trans-ported to medieval Germany. The starkly attractive wooden buildings combine centuries of European tradition with the crudeness of the American frontier. The heavy, sombre single-ness of purpose intended by the founder of the sect, Johann Konrad Beissel, was mitigated for its celibate followers by the fact that music played an important part in their everyday lives. The Cloister was one of the most famous places in the colonies for original religious choral music, and Beissel was one of America's first composers.

The community was also very industrious. They became entirely self-sufficient, boasting — in addition to the appurte-nances of agriculture — a gristmill, a bakery, a pottery, a paper-making factory, and a printing shop. They produced their own religious literature and German translations of English books.

THE PLYMOUTH MEETING FRIENDS' MEETING HOUSE

The Society of Friends (or Quakers) sought the same simplicity that the Dunkers favoured in their own religious buildings, but their architectural forms differed in that they were built from memories of English, rather than German, architecture. The word "Quaker" was first applied to George Fox, an early leader of the Friends, after he advised a magistrate who had just sentenced him to prison to "tremble at the word of the Lord."

What is now the community of Plymouth Meeting, just west of Philadelphia, was settled in 1686 by two prominent English Friends, Francis Rawle and James Fox. They named the location for the last town they saw in their homeland. Later they sold the property to Friends from Wales and moved to Philadelphia. The present stone building (below), built around 1710, was expanded in 1780 to include a school, which is still in operation. In 1867 the building was damaged heavily by fire.

The meetings at the Quaker meeting houses are still based on the principle of silent, direct communication with God, with no pastor, music, or order of service. At these meetings worship is mainly based upon silence, but all are free to speak; from time to time, some participants rise and share their thoughts with the group.

There is a common thread tying together the architectural traditions of the typical Mennonite meeting house near Waterloo, Ontario (opposite), the Cloister of the Seventh Day Dunkers at Ephrata (above), and the meeting house of the Friends at Plymouth Meeting, Pennsylvania (below). None of these sects wanted an elaborate place for worship; the simpler the arrangements were, the better. The Seventh Day Dunkers sat around the table in the *Saal* shown above for their religious services. Early Mennonites and Friends shared accommodation at Germantown, Pennsylvania.

WHITE CHAPEL, PICTON, ONTARIO

Because of Methodism's emphasis on piety, self-sacrifice, industriousness, and moral fervour, it was ideally suited to frontier life. The Methodist church in North America was organized into circuits with itinerant preachers travelling from one settlement to another to carry the word to the pioneers. Protected from the elements by a black woollen cloak and beaver hat, the "circuit rider" went to remote areas where his arrival was awaited eagerly, particularly by those who wished to be married or had children ready to be baptised. The circuit rider's saddle-bags were packed with books which he distributed to

Opposite: a simple log church (top) was built in 1772 at the Moravian town of Schoenbrunn, Ohio, the first post-French settlement in the American Northwest Territory; although the buildings were razed during battles with the Indians, remains of the village have been unearthed and many buildings reconstructed. Below it is the White Chapel, begun in 1809 near Picton, Ontario. It was furnished simply (below) in a style typical of many early Methodist chapels.

those in isolated settlements. He frequently preached out-of-doors when weather permitted. His congregation, knowing few of the comforts of life, were moved to rapture by powerful sermons.

Because outdoor services were not always possible, meeting houses became a necessary part of every community. Most of the early ones were humble structures with little attempt at pretentiousness. Catherine Parr Traill, Ontario's chronicler of pioneer life, wrote in 1832 that "the settlers...invariably adopt whatever plan saves time, labour and money. The great law of expediency is strictly observed; it is born of necessity. Matters of taste appear to be little regarded, or are, at all events, after-considerations."

The White Chapel near Picton (below and opposite, bottom) is one of the few early Methodist meeting houses to have survived. In 1809 a local mill-owner, Stephen Conger, donated the land and the timber for it. The congregation helped pay the construction costs by subscription; many who were without money paid their share in wheat or labour.

BARRATT'S CHAPEL AND ST. ANDREW'S CHURCH

Barratt's Chapel (at the top of this page and the next) has played a significant role in the history of Methodism and is now honoured as one of sixteen historic shrines of the United Methodist Church. On November 14, 1784, the sacrament of the Lord's Supper was first administered in America at this Delaware chapel by an ordained Methodist minister, the Reverend Thomas Coke. Until the end of the American Revolution the Methodists had received the sacraments from ministers of the Anglican church, but with the American victory over the British, rights which had been the sole prerogative of the Church of England were granted to other churches. Coke was sent to America by John Wesley to function as a legal and independent minister. He and the Reverend Francis Asbury met in Barratt's Chapel on that day in November 1784 and made plans to call a conference for all Methodist clergy the following month. At that conference the Methodist Episcopal Church was formed and Barratt's Chapel has thus been referred to as the "cradle of American Methodism."

The building is a fine example of the simple architecture of Methodism. The brick façade is pock-marked with holes that were used to support "putlogs," short timbers that bore the scaffolding during construction. Features inside the church, such as the marble-topped receiving table and the bronze kerosene chandelier (now electrified), date from the Victorian period. The pews are earlier. The bronze star which lies on the floor at the opening in the altar rail marks the spot where the two famous Methodist leaders, Coke and Asbury, first met.

St. Andrew's Presbyterian Church at Williamstown, Ontario (at the bottom of these two pages), is made of French-Canadian uncoursed rubble stonework, but the congregation's British heritage is evident in features such as the windows. The church is an excellent example of the combination of Old- and New-World elements in pioneer architecture.

In the graveyard of St. Andrew's, the style of individual headstones has altered with succeeding generations. While the earliest Canadian settlers marked plots with wooden slabs or roughly shaped stones, an increase in population necessitated community burial grounds and the establishment of stone masonry. Headstones which are dated in the early nineteenth century are most often incised with Roman lettering, but later in the century raised block lettering came into fashion. Decoration became more elaborate with the addition of symbolic depictions of grief, such as shaking hands and weeping willows, but in the early twentieth century there was a return to greater simplicity.

Old Barratt's Chapel (above and opposite, top), one of the oldest Methodist meeting houses in America, was built near Frederica, Delaware, in 1780. St. Andrew's (below and opposite, bottom) was the second Presbyterian church built at Williamstown, Ontario, near Cornwall. It was begun in 1812.

CATHOLICS IN UPPER CANADA AND KENTUCKY

The greatest early leader of the Roman Catholic Scots pioneers was Father Alexander Macdonell, who settled in Ontario's Glengarry County. He organized the Glengarry Fencibles, a regiment that fought gallantly in the War of 1812. In 1821, the year after he was consecrated Roman Catholic Bishop of Upper Canada, Macdonell began work on his followers' largest church, St. Raphael's (above), a sturdy limestone structure that could seat 1,000 worshippers. In 1970 a fire gutted the church, but the ruins were stabilized, and a new smaller church was built adjacent to its shell. St. Raphael's lives on as a landscaped open-air meeting place and concert hall.

It is hard to believe that so grand a building as St. Joseph's Roman Catholic Cathedral at Bardstown, Kentucky (opposite), was built only a few decades after the first Kentucky settlement. But when Bardstown was elevated to an episcopal see in 1808, it required a proper cathedral. Bishop Benedict Joseph Flaget and four young seminarians came to Bardstown, Kentucky, in the spring of 1811. When they arrived, the town contained little more than a group of log houses. One of the newcomers had to sleep "on a tick in the garret" of Flaget's cabin, which "contained no other furniture than a bed, six chairs, two tables, and a few planks for a library." Five years later Bishop Flaget began construction on St. Joseph's Cathedral. Bricks for the walls had to be fired on the site, and stone for the foundations and portico was taken from local quarries.

GREEK AND GOTHIC REVIVAL ARCHITECTURE

Early in the last century, many American artists and architects believed that the imitation of Greek buildings would inspire feelings of democracy in the young nation. Although the Greek Revival was never so strong an element in Canadian architecture, at St. Andrew's Presbyterian Church in Niagara-on-the-Lake, Ontario (on the opposite page), there is a lovely example of the style. Niagara-on-the-Lake was the first town to be settled in Upper Canada, was the first capital of Upper Canada, and is located quite close to the American border — which may have had something to do with the church's design. Such elements as the Georgian tower, however, show the influence of British architecture.

The Gothic Revival, more popular for churches than the Greek Revival, first surfaced in England in the middle of the eighteenth century. Its impact was felt in the New World some time later. Christ Church at Burritt's Rapids, Ontario (above), an Anglican church built in 1831 (the same year as St. An-

drew's), shows the decorative use of the Gothic style in its earlier years. The windows have pointed Gothic arches, the tower a Gothic skyline; but beneath this ornament the general shape and proportions are hardly different from those of St. Andrew's. In both churches the trappings of a revived historical style sit quite superficially on a standard eighteenth-century body.

The plans for the construction of Christ Church were laid by a local committee in response to the prosperity anticipated by the building of the Rideau Waterway. A lock was to be built by the Royal Engineers at Burritt's Rapids and the town looked forward to its completion. Unfortunately, the canal was built primarily to ensure the transport of arms and supplies in the event of an American attack; because the threat of an invasion ceased soon after the canal's completion, the expected prosperity was never attained by the community.

St. Andrew's Presbyterian Church (above and right), built in 1831 at Niagara-on-the-Lake, Ontario, is one of the few Canadian churches to show the influence of the Greek Revival. Christ Church (opposite) was built in the same year at the small town of Burritt's Rapids, Ontario. This Anglican church recalls the Gothic style in its decorative aspects, but in its shape and internal arrangements it resembles earlier American houses of worship.

THE SHARON TEMPLE, ONTARIO

The temple at Sharon, Ontario (on the following page), completed about 1830, was created by David Willson, who left the Society of Friends and started his own religious community called the Children of Peace. Willson was determined to imitate the method of building Solomon's temple. The Davidites worked together for five years, erecting it insofar as possible without modern tools or nails. The Children of Peace once numbered as many as three hundred. When David Willson died in 1866 the group dwindled, and within twenty years had disappeared altogether. The temple and the adjoining study of the founder are preserved today as a museum.

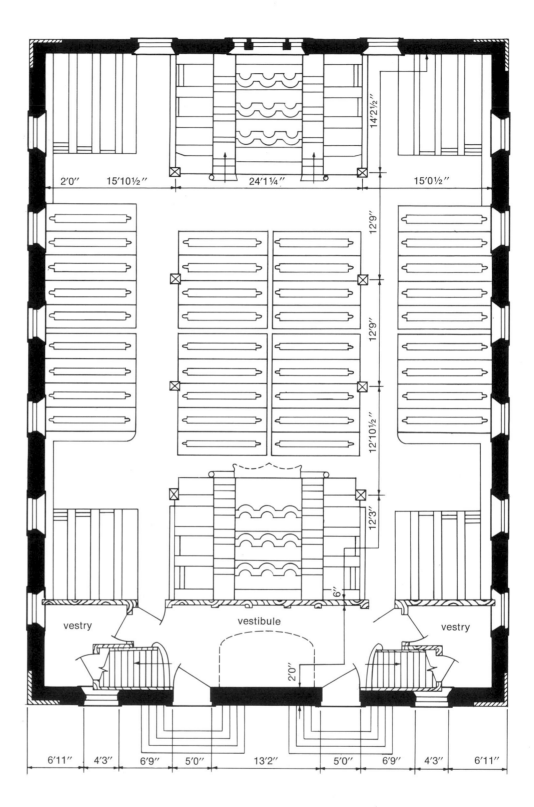

0 4 8 12 16 20 →N

14'2½"

2'0" 15'10½" 24'1¼" 15'0½"

12'9"

12'9"

12'10½"

12'3"

6"

vestry   vestibule   vestry

2'0"

6'11" 4'3" 6'9" 5'0" 13'2" 5'0" 6'9" 4'3" 6'11"

THE TEMPLES OF THE MORMONS

In 1833, Joseph Smith, the founder of the Mormons, had a vision in which he was instructed to build a temple to the Lord. His instructions included detailed plans. This was, he related, as "in ancient days, when the Lord designed a tabernacle or temple should be erected, he spoke to his people, and the Scriptures show that he not only set forth the plan of the building, the length thereof and the breadth thereof, but also the furnishings, the materials, and the very colours to be used."

On the dedication in March, 1836, of the Mormon Temple at Kirtland, Ohio (opposite), there were four days and nights of emotional excitement, including many signs and wonders, heavenly music, and a pillar of fire hovering over the temple. The church has three storeys: the ground, or "Church" floor, for public worship; the upper "Apostolic" storey, for the instruction of the priesthood; and school rooms fill the attic. Above is the plan for the first floor of the temple. The Mormons were driven out of Kirtland and settled for a time in Illinois, before being forced westward to Utah.

Expanding the Frontier

Until late in the 1700s the westward expansion of the Thirteen Colonies was halted by a British proclamation forbidding settlement west of the Appalachian watershed, as well as by the much more intimidating barrier of the Appalachian Mountains themselves. But the time eventually came when the coastal plains became crowded. If the people wanted land, it had to be to the west. A new generation of pioneers began moving south into what is now West Virginia and western North Carolina, and then northwest to confront the mountain passes that led to the interior.

In the years before and during the American Revolutionary War the proclamation banning settlement came to be honoured

This gallery at the Cane Ridge Meeting House (left) was filled to capacity in August, 1801, when the Reverend Barton W. Stone led the great Kentucky revival. Between 10,000 and 30,000 people flocked to Cane Ridge from all over Kentucky and Ohio. For a week they eagerly listened to the preachers; by night, as hundreds of campfires lit up the countryside, miracles were seen to happen. About 3,000 converted and formed the nucleus of the group now generally known as the Disciples of Christ. Below is an exterior view of the meeting house. Opposite: The interior of the Moravian Meeting House, Schoenbrunn, Ohio.

more in the breach than the observance, and pioneers trickled across the mountain barrier. In 1787, when the new American government opened the west with an ordinance whose first article guaranteed settlers religious freedom, the trickle became a torrent. Settlers first reached Kentucky and Tennessee, then spread into the newly created Northwest Territory (those lands that were to become Ohio, Indiana, Illinois, Michigan, Wisconsin, and a part of Minnesota) as far west as the Mississippi River. They arrived in large numbers in what were to become the Canadian provinces of Ontario and (to a lesser extent) Quebec.

Cane Ridge, Kentucky, a favourite hunting place of long hunter Daniel Boone, was a settlement in the cane brake region north of Boonesborough and Harrodsburg, about fifteen miles northeast of Lexington. Presbyterian minister Robert W. Finley and his newly arrived followers built a meeting house there that is typical of log structures of pioneer America: squared logs were set upon a stone foundation and held together at the corners with notched ends; mud chinking was packed into the crevices between the logs to keep out drafts; heavy trusses rest upon the walls and support the roof, with its long oaken shakes. Oak was used also for the floor. A ladder propped up against the outside wall leads to a large gallery.

The log cabin – and by extension the log church – is often regarded as the prime symbol of the American frontier. Such buildings were actually a European – probably a Swedish and then a German – importation, unknown to the Indians. By the eighteenth century log structures had appeared everywhere on the American frontier and knew few geographical or chronological boundaries.

In the mid-nineteenth century the people of Kitley Township in Ontario built a small log structure to be used by any itinerant minster who might come to bring them the word of God. Now located in Upper Canada Village, a reconstructed pioneer town near Cornwall, Ontario, Providence Church is typical of the first house of worship built in most frontier communities between the later years of the eighteenth century and the early years of the twentieth. The log church was an expedient solution to a pressing need; the pioneers were indifferent to appearance. The permanent churches that followed when neither time nor money was in such acutely short supply were frequently seen as image-makers; the early temporary churches, never.

The plainness of Providence Church and its bare interior, furnished only with a high pulpit, may also derive from the vital influence of Methodism on Ontario frontier society. Methodism's founder, John Wesley, espoused rigid ecclesiastical methods which later gave his sect its name. Throughout the middle of the eighteenth century, Wesley's associate George Whitefield made seven incredibly successful evangelical tours of America. His emotional preaching brought crowds to tears, led them to confess their sins, and often made them faint. Wesley and Whitefield urged churches to adopt simple doctrines, and their own preference for simple house-like chapels likely influenced the builders of Providence Church.

The Methodists were often unfairly denounced as fanatics

The settlers of Kitley Township, Ontario, worried about the cost of building a church. They were assured by one Granny Good that "Providence will provide." When funds for the church materialized, it was named to commemorate Granny Good's prediction.

by members of the older, more established religions. Major-General Isaac Brock, Administrator of Upper Canada, condemned the Methodists as a dangerous element, "highly prejudicial to the peace of Society." Brock was reacting to the heavy influx of Methodists from the American states, which made them numerically the largest religious group in the Canadian province. Members of the older sects – people like General Brock – showed their disdain for the Methodists' primitive meeting houses when they built more imposing and traditional churches for themselves.

The first Methodist meeting houses in Canada were built in 1792 in the Bay of Quinte circuit along the northern shore of Lake Ontario. One meeting house from this early period survives – the White Chapel, or Conger Chapel, near Picton, Ontario, begun in 1809. As with other churches in the area, the presence of a sawmill meant that the White Chapel could be built of a timber frame covered with siding. The primitive technology of the earliest years was being replaced with more complex building methods. The day of the log church ended

when water-powered sawmills went into operation.

The White Chapel is nearly square, with a second tier of windows illuminating the balcony. It resembles the earlier American Methodist meeting houses. Like those buildings, it is similar to the even older Congregational meeting house of New England. Methodism, like Congregationalism before it, was a young denomination, with few ties to earlier liturgies or building types. It was primarily a preaching religion. The simplicity of the Methodist chapel was appropriate to the "primitive" (as its practitioners called it) nature of the service that went on within.

Canadian Methodism was imported from the American states to the south; Presbyterianism arrived directly from its country of origin with the emigration of large numbers of Highlanders around the year 1800. Many Scots, fleeing depressed economic conditions at home, settled in Upper Canada along the St. Lawrence River above Montreal. The first Presbyterian clergyman in Upper Canada, an energetic dominie from the Isle of Skye named John Bethune, founded the province's first con-

Methodists built the cobblestone West Dumfries Chapel at Paris Plains, Ontario, in 1845. The stones are set in neat courses (below).

gregation at Williamstown, north of Cornwall. In the fashion of so many North American pioneers of all times and places, the Williamstown settlers first built a temporary log church; but, beginning in 1812, they replaced it with a stone kirk that was completed six years later. The new St. Andrew's Church is simple in form but impressive in stature, effectively combining the Old World and the New. The walls were built of uncoursed rubble stonework by French mason François-Xavier Rochileaux in the traditional Québecois manner. British elements such as the Palladian arches framing the windows were added by John Kirby, who took charge of construction upon Rochileaux's premature death.

The first Scottish Roman Catholic pioneers in Upper Canada were United Empire Loyalists from the United States who arrived in 1783 or 1784. They were joined a few years later by another 500 settlers – mostly Macdonells – who emigrated directly from the Scottish Highlands. They named their new home Glengarry County, after the Glengarry they had left.

At St. Andrew's West – a contracted form of the original

"St. Andrew's, Canada West" – these Scots built a church of logs. It measured eighteen feet by twenty-four feet, scarcely larger than a present-day living room. The foundation – a single course of stones held together with mortar – was unearthed in 1938. By 1801 the settlers had replaced their log church with a stone structure of much larger dimensions. Its eastern end is rounded in the tradition of Catholic churches; the shape is common in the churches of Quebec. This building was replaced in the middle years of the nineteenth century. It survives today, with its former steep roof lowered, as a parish hall.

English pioneers, as well as Scots, infused early Canada with the British tradition. The most militant British clergyman to come to the colony was Jacob Mountain, the first Anglican bishop of Quebec, a man who devoted his episcopate to trying (in vain) to make the Church of England the established religion in French and Roman Catholic Quebec. When Mountain assumed his duties the Anglican minority of Quebec, most of whom had arrived very recently as United Empire Loyalists, had no church of their own. They worshipped in the Récollet Chapel until it was destroyed by fire in 1796, whereupon they used the Jesuit Chapel, which Mountain complained was "in all respects insufficient for our purpose, small, dark, dirty, and ill-suited to receive a decent assembly of people." He petitioned to England for funds to build a new church, arguing that "nothing, I believe, would tend more effectually to give weight and consequence to the Establishment than a proper Church at Quebec, exclusively appropriated to our Worship."

Permission and money were granted, and in 1800 construction began on Holy Trinity Cathedral. The church – like Mountain's episcopate – was patterned upon an English model. It was designed and constructed by Englishmen (directed by master mason Edward Cannon) and built to a small degree of English materials. The architects were Major William Robe and Captain Hall of the Royal Artillery; their design – like that of all pioneer churches – was inspired by the architecture of their homeland, but was determined by the conditions in the new country. "The general dimensions of this church," wrote Major Robe, "were in great measure taken from those of St. Martin-in-the-Fields [James Gibbs' masterpiece in Trafalgar Square, London], but the state of materials and workmanship in Canada made a plain design necessary." Robe further explained that details of the design were appropriated as well from the ancient Roman architecture of Vitruvius and the Pantheon, and from the Renaissance Italians Alberti, Vignola, and Palladio.

For Robe and his generation, English architecture was simply the latest stage in a long tradition of classical design going back to antiquity. St. Martin-in-the-Fields was the best known of the early eighteenth-century London churches. The publication of the plans for it by architect Gibbs in his popular *Book of Architecture* had inspired numerous pre-Revolutionary American churches. Robe and Hall dusted off the volume a generation after the more sophisticated American architects had tired of it (as they had of British political rule).

When the Cathedral of the Holy Trinity is compared to its English prototype, it is evident that something has been lost – or gained – in translation. The basic external form remains rectangular, with a temple front surmounted by a tall spire, but the details differ. All has been simplified to put less strain on the colony's funds, its pool of talent, and its simpler architectural taste. St. Martin's grand portico of eight Corinthian columns has become a flattened façade of four Ionic pilasters. Major Robe confessed that "the pilasters project less than Palladio's rule directs, owing to the Pointe-aux-Trembles stone, which, in the then state of the quarries, could not be got in masses large enough without an enormous expense." Paperthin arches between the pilasters only hint at St. Martin's deep porch. The interior, however, follows the prototype much more closely.

Explorer Simon Fraser and John Sandfield Macdonald, first premier of Ontario, are buried beside St. Andrew's West church.

Architect James Gibbs' design for St. Martin-in-the-Fields, London, England.

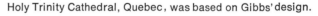

Holy Trinity Cathedral, Quebec, was based on Gibbs' design.

In spite of many changes, the Quebec church is clearly derived from St. Martin-in-the-Fields. The new cathedral is a true pioneer church, based directly on an idea from the mother country yet altered by the conditions of the colonial locale. The inspiration was of the Old World; the execution was of the New.

When Bishop Mountain chose the site and built the home for his see, Quebec had, of course, been settled for two centuries and had a highly developed culture. Mountain and his Anglican flock were not pioneers in an alien wilderness; they considered themselves pioneers in an alien culture. The small parish churches of Mountain's diocese were consequently also self-consciously English in design.

One of the loveliest is the church of St. Stephen's at Chambly, Quebec, some fifteen miles east of Montreal. For much of its history, Chambly has been a fort town, at different times held by French, English, and American troops. The Anglican church was built in 1820 to serve the garrison; it mattered little that the English-speaking townspeople were mostly Scottish Presbyterians.

Unknown to him, Bishop Mountain had a kindred spirit some thousand miles to the southwest, in the person of Bishop Benedict Joseph Flaget. Flaget, like Mountain, sought to assert his faith in an alien environment and he recognized the power of strong architectural statement. But whereas Mountain had been an Anglican in a sea of Catholics, Flaget was a Roman Catholic in a land filled with Protestants. Born in France, Flaget came to America in 1792 and became the parish priest in the

St. Stephen's Anglican Church at Chambly, Quebec, looks much like a rural English Georgian church. It combines *Québecois* rubble stonework with the English prototype.

French town of Vincennes, Indiana, the oldest white settlement in that western territory. Flaget was soon recalled to Baltimore, the centre of Catholic activity in the United States. When in 1808 the episcopal see of Bardstown, Kentucky, was formed to include the whole Northwest Territory, Flaget went there to become its first bishop.

Bardstown was a recent settlement on the Wilderness Road, some forty miles west of Harrodsburg. When the town found itself at the head of a diocese, a simple log chapel dedicated to St. Joseph was hastily promoted to the rank of cathedral. A few years later it was succeeded by a building hardly more impressive: a larger log house in the Seminary of St. Thomas. Bishop Flaget resolved to erect a proper church, and so in 1816 he laid the cornerstone of St. Joseph's Cathedral in Bardstown.

Baltimore architect John Rogers followed the same Gibbsian model of St. Martin-in-the-Fields as had Bishop Mountain's builders in Quebec — here for a Catholic rather than an Anglican church. The reason for Rogers' source must lie in the determination to build a cathedral that was impressive rather than necessarily overtly Catholic; the Gibbs tradition was still followed in the architecturally less progressive regions of America. The Bardstown cathedral boasts a grand portico with six free-standing Ionic columns. A splendid spire rises to a height of about 150 feet (the same as Holy Trinity in Quebec City). Its elaborately designed and detailed interior belies the fact that it was built in a territory which had received its first settlers only a few years before.

Bishop Flaget did not forget his former parishioners at Vincennes. He directed that the old log church in which he had served be replaced by a more worthy church building modelled after the Bardstown cathedral. The basic form is indeed the same, but the portico has been omitted, giving the building a much more French appearance and reflecting the French heritage of the area.

The Indiana church, which was to become the Cathedral of St. Francis Xavier, was modelled on one in Kentucky, which took its source from a design once popular along the eastern seaboard. As the pioneers moved west, they brought with them the building types with which they had been familiar — just as a century or two earlier the new arrivals along the coast had followed European models.

This migration of architectural forms can also be seen by following the tracks of the New Englanders who moved westward to the Ohio country. New Englanders felt an affinity for what they called their Western Reserve. The pioneers brought their building practices with them, and as a result many Ohio

Top left: The nave of St. Joseph's Cathedral, Bardstown, Kentucky, is flanked by eight columns, each hewn from one poplar trunk, plastered, and painted to imitate marble. Top, right: St. Francis Xavier Cathedral, Vincennes, Indiana, begun in 1826, took twenty-five years to complete. Opposite: The Old Colony Church, Bishop Hill, Illinois, was the first permanent building erected by a Swedish communistic community led by Eric Janson. The lower floor is divided into sleeping rooms; the upper storey contains the church.

Remembrance of Things Past

The Congregational Church in Tallmadge, Ohio, was built by pioneers from Connecticut.

The pioneers who opened the interior of the continent in the second quarter of the nineteenth century came with a new attitude towards architecture. Whereas previous pioneers had often simply transferred the familiar structures of the homeland to the new environment, this new generation perceived architecture – especially church architecture – as a statement of ideals, which sprang from a carefully premeditated examination of architectural alternatives. Often the final choice was dictated by architectural movements in Europe; just as often, the choice was uniquely North American, either in its selection or rejection of past styles. All of the choices, however, were a product of the Romantic Movement, which inspired the cultivation of personal intuitions and feelings.

In architecture, the Romantic spirit embodied a love of symbolism and a love of the remote. These sentiments inspired architectural revivals which from this time forward went hand in hand with new settlement. The Greek Revival style was one of the first to accompany nineteenth-century pioneers across an awakening continent. To these settlers, classicism was not a modern style which had developed and changed over the centuries from a long and continuous tradition, as it had been to the builders at Quebec, Bardstown, and Tallmadge; rather, it was an old style to be revived after long disuse. To Americans, it symbolized the establishment of a magnificent new civilization on this continent, modelled after the ancient democracies of Greece and Rome in their days of glory.

The Second Presbyterian Church in Madison, Indiana, was built in 1834-1835 in a newly settled, but architecturally sophisticated, Ohio River town. It uses ancient Greek architectural forms in this new way. Architect Edwin J. Peck places columns

hamlets hardly differ in appearance from the New England towns from which their residents had come.

The village of Tallmadge (today a suburb of Akron) was laid out by the Reverend David Bacon, a New England minister who hoped to establish a self-governing Congregational community in the Ohio wilderness. Bacon formed an oval village green with eight radial roads that lead to the farmland beyond. The town's church was built on the green in 1821. Architect-builder Lemuel Porter was himself from Connecticut.

The building is almost indistinguishable from Connecticut Congregational churches of the same period. The Ohio church, like its Connecticut counterparts, relies upon classical forms for its ornament. The columns of the porch and spire and the entablatures, pediments, and cornices that they support – indeed, just about all of the decoration — imitate the architecture of Georgian England, which looked back to that of Renaissance Italy, and which, in turn, had been inspired by the buildings of ancient Rome. The cathedrals at Bardstown and Quebec were likewise products of this heritage. They do not resemble any particular buildings from antiquity; they were conceived as modern designs that continued a long classical tradition.

The First Methodist Church, Taylors Falls, Minnesota, retains simplified Greek Revival features.

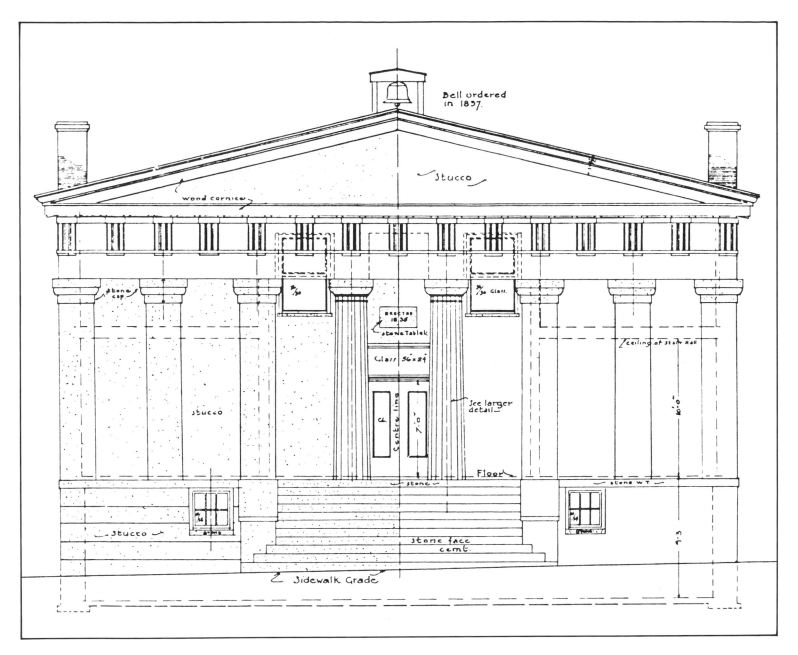

A drawing of Second Presbyterian Church, Madison, Indiana, which was completed in 1835. It reveals the church's classical proportions.

topped by a pediment across the front of the building, as had Lemuel Porter at Tallmadge, but here with a different effect. The source is now a particular building type from the ancient world: the Greek Doric temple. The compact silhouette, with its unbroken lines and low gabled roof, imitates the temple profile. The eight Greek Doric columns (six are actually square piers) specifically recall the façade of the famed Parthenon in Athens.

The symbolism lies in the associative value of the Greek temple. The American building is in no way a direct copy – the walls are of stuccoed brick, not marble; columns line one façade instead of four; and the interiors of the modern and the ancient building are utterly different. But it is an evocative statement meant to kindle romantic associations in the observer. It appealed to the emotions and sentiments of nineteenth-century Americans, as did the cheaper cost of so simple a structure.

Peck's contemporary, architect Robert Mills, was the first native American trained as an architect and was largely responsible for the Greek Revival character of Washington, DC. He wrote of the revival: "It was fortunate that this style was so early introduced into our country, both on the ground of economy and of correct taste, as it exactly suited the character of our political institutions and pecuniary means."

As the pioneers forged further west, their buildings at times became simpler in form. The First Methodist Church at Taylors Falls, Minnesota, built in 1860, retains the temple form; but the Methodist spirit of simplicity has reduced its columns to the thinnest of pilasters, the mouldings to the barest suggestion of classical form. Fine carpentry produced particularly handsome, clean lines.

The Greek Revival never caught on in Canada as in the United States, in part because Canadians never made such a fuss about democracy. One church that does, however, show Greek Revival influence is St. Andrew's Presbyterian Church at Niagara-on-the-Lake, Ontario, the attractive border town that was rebuilt after having been put to the torch by American forces during the War of 1812. The design, executed in 1831, follows the Wren-Gibbs tradition perpetuated in the builders' pattern books of the day.

The ancient Greeks were but one of the nations whose buildings were admired by the nineteenth-century Romantics. The architects of the period culled ideas from just about every past architectural style. It was the Gothic Revival that had the greatest effect upon church architecture. The Gothic period of the European Middle Ages – that is, the era between about

Notre Dame in Montreal was once the largest church north of Mexico.

The church's interior was remodelled fifty years after construction.

the twelfth and fifteenth centuries – had been a time of prolific church building. The spiky, irregular Gothic style is a delight to the eye and provided nineteenth-century people with a picturesque reflection of their own history. To pioneers in an alien wilderness, a sense of historical presence was a precious thing, providing something of security, identity, and comfort. In their zeal to recreate Europe in the wilderness, they were quick to latch onto the Gothic Revival style.

The first Gothic Revival church building in North America was the work of a French refugee-architect, Maximilien Godefroy. He arrived in Baltimore in 1805 to teach architecture and fine arts at St. Mary's College, an academy recently established by Sulpician monks who were themselves refugees from France. Three months later he designed a new chapel for the college's sister seminary. He designed a building containing all the Gothic features worthy of imitation, yet one which looks not one whit like an authentic Gothic building.

Every element of St. Mary's Chapel reminds the visitor of Gothic architecture: the tall spire over the entrance (never erected), the pointed finials at each corner, the decorated pointed arched openings of the door and its flanking windows, the row of statues placed in the niches above (carved by a sculptor seconded from the Capitol in Washington), the circular rose window, and the thin wall buttresses.

Fifteen years after the completion of St. Mary's Chapel the Sulpicians of Montreal resolved to rebuild their venerable church of Notre Dame – the place of worship for the parish of Montreal and the Seminary of St. Sulpice – in the same Gothic revival style. Architect James O'Donnell, an Irish Protestant from New York, built a church that was for fifty years the largest church north of Mexico. Its twin towers, triple-arched doorway, and consistent use of Gothic decoration reminded Montrealers of Notre Dame in Paris. Like St. Mary's Chapel, however, it had essentially a Georgian body clad in Gothic dress.

A few Anglican and Episcopalian churches – mostly in Canada – began to adopt elements of the Gothic Revival in the 1820s, at about the same time as the construction of Notre Dame. One of the earliest British North American buildings in the style was St. John's church in Saint John, New Brunswick, begun in 1824. The somewhat sombre building, known as The Stone Church, was designed by local architect Lloyd Johnston. Rector Robert Willis described the church as being "of rough stone, and of the Gothic order." The stone had been quarried in England and used as ballast on the voyage to Canada.

A few years later, the Loyalist settlers of the small Ontario community of Burritt's Rapids met in their school house to make plans "for the purpose of erecting a house of public worship for the established church of England exclusively." The congregation did not discuss the style of their church, but they did debate its material. Twelve members, including the Reverend Henry Patton, voted for wood; five opted in vain for more expensive stone. The third alternative, brick, received no support.

Christ Church, as the attractive wood building came to be called, stands today much as it did on its completion in 1831. Its rectangular plan and tall entrance tower differ little from so many of the churches that had been erected in America in earlier times. The building revives the Gothic style, but only in its decorative elements: the elegant pointed windows and doorway, and the notched crenellations and pointed pinnacles atop the tower (which also sports classically derived quoins). The interior treatment is similar, with three elegant pointed arches separating nave from chancel.

Christ Church Cathedral in Fredericton, New Brunswick, was one building whose design resulted from a completely altered attitude toward the Gothic style. A group of English theologians who sought to revive old church forms began in the second quarter of the nineteenth century to publish a monthly magazine called *The Ecclesiologist*, named for their society, which offered criticism (often unsolicited) to church builders. Their doctrine resolved that "Gothick is the only true Christian architecture."

The Ecclesiologists did not invent the Gothic Revival, they canonized it. In the 1820s the question had been whether or not to use Gothic; a generation later one asked which kind of Gothic to use. And the ecclesiologists made no bones about preferring the Decorated phase of the fourteenth century. As a result of their activities, churches henceforth would recall the Gothic style in their shape and internal arrangement as well as in decoration.

The Ecclesiologist directly pressured the Right Reverend John Medley, first Bishop of New Brunswick, to make his church conform to its version of the Gothic style. Medley had arrived in Fredericton in 1845 and had immediately set to work building his new cathedral. When *The Ecclesiologist* got wind of the fact that he planned to model his cathedral on an English parish church, the editors reported that they could only "grieve that so well-meant, so noble an attempt at better things, should not embody all those characteristic features of an English cathedral." Medley relented, and with the assistance of the respected English architect, William Butterfield, he completed Christ Church Cathedral in a manner that *The Ecclesiologist* called a "great improvement." The long chancel and its high roof are appropriate to the High Church service. In keeping with the dignity of a cathedral, the clerestory windows were made more traditional in design. The product is an impressively handsome stone structure that almost looks as if it could have been built in medieval England.

Christ Church Cathedral is truly a church in the Gothic Revival style, whereas Christ Church at Burritt's Rapids had merely been one with Gothic decoration. Both are products of the Gothic *Revival,* as opposed to seventeenth-century buildings such as the Old Brick Church in Isle of Wight County, Virginia (mentioned in the Introduction), which is an example of a Gothic *Survival.*

Smaller churches also fell under the influence of the ecclesiologists. One of the most attractive wooden Episcopalian churches in the later-settled territories is St. John Chrysostom in Delafield, Wisconsin. Construction was begun in 1851, some five years after Wisconsin achieved statehood. Some say that

The tower of St. John's Anglican Church, Saint John, New Brunswick.

plans for the church were provided by Richard Ralston Cox, a young missionary from Philadelphia who had helped organize the congregation. The church was partly dedicated to his memory after he was killed in a steamboat accident on the Ohio River. Another tradition attributes the design to the country's most famous church architect, Richard Upjohn, a devoted High Churchman and designer of Trinity Church in New York. Both reports are to a certain extent true.

The compact design of St. John Chrysostom, with its low walls and steep Gothic roof, was inspired by the stone church of St. James the Less, Philadelphia, a virtual copy of the thirteenth-century church of St. Michael's, Long Stanton, Cambridgeshire. St. James' was the first church in the United States to be erected under the direct supervision of the English ecclesiologists, who recommended this simpler Early English style for colonial builders lacking in funds and building skills. Cox realized that the expensive and difficult stone construction of the Philadelphia church was inappropriate for the pioneer carpenters of Wisconsin. He adapted the silhouette of St. James the Less to the system of frame construction being popularized for churches by Richard Upjohn. The latter was in the midst of publishing his immensely popular *Upjohn's Rural Architecture,* which sought "to supply the want which is felt, especially in the newly settled parts of our country, of designs for cheap

but still substantial buildings for the use of parishes." Although the volume had not yet appeared when sod was broken for St. John Chrysostom, a letter in Upjohn's business correspondence reveals that his office may have sent a plan to the Wisconsin congregation.

St. John Chrysostom is a Carpenter's Gothic church, based on the design of an English Gothic parish church and built in a wholly American system of wood construction. Inside, the simple and handsome natural wood finish is complemented by beautiful hand-wrought hardware (forged by local blacksmith Jacob Luther) and by superb leaded glass windows. In keeping with the new liturgy derived from the return to earlier church practices, the chancel is separated from the nave by a rood screen. The pulpit stands along one side, as it had been in earlier Anglican churches; the ecclesiologists insisted that a pulpit in the middle of the aisle was a feature of a mere preaching house.

The Wisconsin builders erected no spire, following St.

Top left: The original design for Christ Church Cathedral, Fredericton, New Brunswick. Bottom left: The final result. Below: the interior of Christ Church Cathedral. Opposite: Richard Upjohn's "Design for a Wooden Church" (1852), created for pioneer congregations in rural areas.

Michael's and St. James the Less. Perhaps fearing that a small belfry of wood might be insecure, they placed the bell in a separate structure just west of the church.

Board-and-batten siding had been urged for all wood building in the books of influential designer Andrew Jackson Downing. He preferred vertical boarding to horizontal "because it has an expression of strength and truthfulness which the other has not," and because "it better expresses the picturesque – a kind of beauty essentially belonging to wooden houses." The Ecclesiological Society was never very fond of wood, but conceded that vertical siding might be appropriate for some churches in the New World. Whether for houses or for churches, this was a method of construction peculiarly suited to the North American climate, conditions, and tastes. In combination with a European-inspired plan, it provided yet another paradigm of pioneer building.

The Gothic Revival increased in popularity as the century progressed. Before long all Christian denominations adopted it for their churches. (Later chapters will trace the movement of the style across the continent.) In its earliest years, however, the Gothic Revival remained primarily the mode of the Roman Catholics and Anglo-Catholics, while other denominations preferred the various classical styles. Revivalism of one sort or the other was the order of the day.

A third path was chosen by the various separatist sects who did not want to be identified with any of the established religions. They sought designs that might reflect their uniqueness and avoid an imitation of either Gothic or Greek. In southern Ontario stands a building erected by such a group: Sharon Temple, home of the Children of Peace. They were the followers of David Willson – and hence known as Davidites – a native of upper New York state who had crossed Lake Ontario and joined the Society of Friends. A mystical experience inspired Willson to speak out loudly at a monthly meeting of the Friends; when he continued his disruptive ways at the next meeting he was expelled from the society. He and five other families withdrew from the Quakers and established themselves at Sharon as the Children of Peace. They and their followers deviated from the established group in such practices as their love of music, their intricate service, and the observance of feast days (most notably Thanksgiving).

In 1825 a message instructed Willson to erect a temple. He appealed to his associates for assistance:

> Oh! friends and workmen, come to me,
>   If you accept the plan,
> We'll build a throne of liberty,
>   An equal rest for man.

As Upjohn recommended, the timber frame of St. John Chrysostom Church in Delafield, Wisconsin, has vertical board-and-batten siding.

Willson had no experience in architecture, yet with the help of master builder Ebenezer Doan he directed his followers to erect a structure that is both handsome and rich in symbolism. The building is sited on a level plain, enclosed by a fence and then by a row of maple trees. The temple itself is sixty feet square in plan – representing "square dealing with all the world" – and its three tiers stand for the Trinity. Four doors face the four compass points, because people from all points of the compass were expected to come to worship. Forty windows, each divided on the three levels into seventy-two, sixty, and fifty-four panes of glass respectively, flood the interior with light. One row of interior columns bears the names of the apostles; other posts with this square are designated "Faith," "Hope," "Love," and "Charity." The ground floor was used for worship, the second storey as a musicians' gallery. At the top, more than seventy feet above the ground, clusters of pinnacles and a gilded ball inscribed "Peace" reach toward the heavens.

The Davidite sect survived its founder by only a few years. A religious group of much more lasting significance is the Church of Jesus Christ of Latter-Day Saints, commonly known as the Mormons. Joseph Smith, the original leader of the sect, had a revelation in his eighteenth year in which the angel Moroni appeared to him three times and directed him to a volume of gold plates inscribed in a strange tongue. Smith dictated a translation of the plates, published in 1830 as *The Book of Mormon*. In the same year the new church was organized at Fayette, New York, with Smith its prophet.

The sect was gradually forced westward, driven on by disapproving citizens wherever they settled. An early convert from Ohio, Sidney Rigdon, was instrumental in bringing the

Mormons to that state, which had been guaranteed religious freedom by the Northwest Ordinance. Smith and fifty families joined Rigdon's one hundred members and settled in the town of Kirtland. There the prophet established a general store, sawmill, and tannery, and planned a great city.

On May 6, 1833, Joseph Smith had a vision in which he was instructed that a temple should be built and was shown "a pattern of the building with dimensions." Work began immediately on the erection of the Kirtland Temple, the first religious building erected by the Mormons. Every evening Smith instructed master builder Joseph Bump with his duties for the following day. Each member of the church contributed labour. Smith himself was foreman in the quarry, and the elders all assisted. Those who had teams of oxen hauled the stone, bringing to the building site in one day a supply that lasted the masons a week. Sidney Rigdon laboured as a mason, and future Mormon leader Brigham Young, a painter and glazier by training, worked on the interior. The temple took three years to build.

The building is about sixty feet by eighty feet in size, with rubble sandstone trimmed in cut stone and covered wth stucco. Embedded in the stucco is broken glass collected by the women and used to make the walls sparkle. Smith and his builders – most of whom had been Protestant New Englanders – followed the basic forms of the Congregational churches with which they were familiar. A comparison with the nearby church at Tallmadge shows that both are rectangular structures two storeys high (the temple has a third floor disguised within its roof), with a pediment surmounted by a tower at the entrance end. The temple, however, follows no consistent decorative style; the two rows of windows are pointed in the Gothic manner; the large end windows are Georgian; the interior mouldings are mostly Greek; and the quoins have no prototype at all.

Two doors lead into the temple, one probably intended for each sex, as in the Friends' meeting houses with which Smith was familiar. Separate but similar halls occupy the two storeys. Each of the two auditoriums has tiers of pulpits at each end in ascending rows of three. The eastern pulpits were used by the Aaronic priesthood, the western ones by the higher Melchisidek priesthood. Moveable pews and curtains on rollers permit partitioning and flexible usage. The interior is superbly finished with fine mouldings and carved woodwork. Every surface received skilled and loving care.

Ohio failed to provide the Mormons with the secure home that they sought. Smith and Rigdon were tarred and feathered shortly before the temple was begun. Harrassment later became worse and in 1838, only two years after the completion of the temple, the town of Kirtland was abandoned. It remained empty for many years, eventually being taken over by the reorganized Church of Jesus Christ of Latter-Day Saints, a neo-Mormon group led by the grandson of Joseph Smith.

After leaving Kirtland the Mormons found temporary homes in Missouri and then Illinois, where Smith and his brother were killed by an angry mob. Brigham Young succeeded Smith and led the group to the safety of Utah, joining hundreds of other pioneers trekking across Prairies and Plains and through mountain passes to the west coast.

St. John's Episcopalian Church at Eolia, Missouri, was built by settlers from Virginia. It is similar to Merchant's Hope Church (page 66) in Prince George County, Virginia, in materials and design.

PLAINS SETTLERS FROM ICELAND
AND RUSSIA

Large numbers of Scandinavians poured onto the Plains on both sides of the border. A mass migration from Iceland began in the 1870s and brought 30,000 people – one-third the entire population – to America in thirty years. They settled around Lake Winnipeg and took up fishing, as they had back home. At his new Manitoba home, the Reverend Pall Thorlaksson held onto a long-standing dream of forming an Icelandic community in the United States. In 1879-1880 a large number of Manitoba Icelanders followed him south to the area around Pembina, North Dakota. Alarmed at the prospect of losing settlers from the thinly populated territory, the Canadian government tried in vain to stop them.

More Icelanders arrived in North Dakota from the homeland and from Minnesota. A strong community developed around Pembina, a town that had begun as a North West Company trading post. Thorlaksson's congregation established the Icelandic Lutheran Church at Gardar and in 1887 built their first church (above).

Many German minority groups had settled in Russia in the late eighteenth and early nineteenth centuries when the czars offered them religious freedom and free land. In the 1870s Czar Alexander II withdrew the Germans' privileges. Persecution followed and their migrations began again. Those who left Russia for America included Mennonites, Roman Catholics, Jews, and Ukrainians.

The Mennonites began to come to Manitoba in 1874; within three years, 7,000 had arrived. They organized into small farm villages, building their characteristic houses with attached barns. The Mennonite "Plain People" became self-sufficient and avoided intercourse with the rest of society. Churches were built at intervals, often serving a number of villages. The Mennonite Church at the Mennonite Village Museum at Steinbach, Manitoba (opposite, top and bottom) was built in 1881.

Above: The Icelandic Lutheran Church at Gardar, North Dakota, near Pembina. Opposite, top and bottom: The Mennonite Church at the Mennonite Village Museum at Steinbach, Manitoba, used to serve a pioneer community at Winkler. It was built by German-speaking refugees from Russian persecution, who were lured to Manitoba by Canadian immigration agents in 1874. Such immigration agents co-operated with the Canadian Pacific Railway – as they had with American railroads.

146

THE RED RIVER SETTLEMENT, MANITOBA

The settlement of the Red River valley was organized by Thomas Douglas, the Fifth Earl of Selkirk, who brought to Canada Scottish crofters who were driven off the land in the early nineteenth century. The first settlers faced scurvy in their first winter and a drought in the first summer. They lacked the necessary tools and seeds, and internal dissent weakened their ranks. They named their colony Kildonan, after the parish in the northern tip of Scotland from which many had come. They built log houses along the river, adapted to the new agricultural conditions, and learned to hunt. The tightly knit community spoke Gaelic and retained their Presbyterian faith. Before sailing from Scotland, the first settlers had stipulated that a minister accompany them. None came, and so an elder was given the authority to baptize and marry. They were to wait forty years for the first minister of their faith; this, they maintained, was a misfortune even greater than those they encountered on first arriving. The first Presbyterian church at the settlement was Old Kildonan (right).

The first Anglican church at the settlement was St. John's (above). The limestone for St. Andrew's Anglican Church (opposite) was quarried on the banks of the river; chief mason Duncan McRae – a Kildonan Scot – cut it into large blocks and built the walls. The wooden floors were hand sawn from trees felled nearby; the glass, paint, putty, nails, and bells came all the way from England.

Above: St. John's Church, built in 1823 by John West, was Anglican by denomination but serviced Presbyterians for a time. Right: Old Kildonan Church (1853) was the first Presbyterian church built in the Red River settlement. Opposite: St. Andrew's Church (1849) was the most attractive Anglican church there. On the following page: McDougall United Church, Morley, Alberta. Its founder thought the site would become "the favourite resort of the tourist."

TWO PLAINS CHURCHES

While the valleys of mid-continent North America were being
settled, the Great Plains of the United States and Canada continued to pose an almost impenetrable barrier to the settlers.
The vast, treeless land extends two thousand miles north from
Texas to Alberta. It has an average width of four hundred miles
between the fertile Mississippi valley and the Rocky Mountains
in the United States, and almost twice that in Canada. Early
explorers flatly declared the land unsuitable for settlement.

Trails across the Prairies began to open in the 1840s and
large caravans used them to reach the western coast; but the
turning point came in the 1860s, when the promise of cheap or
even free land lured settlers to remain in these "deserts." Advances in farming techniques and the coming of the railroad
made the possibility of settlement in the area a more inviting
prospect. Pioneers from the east continued to pour into the
Plains and, as in eastern settlements, they built churches where
they settled.

A very primitive church was built at Phoenix, Arizona
(top). Its frame consisted of cottonwood tree trunks set at
intervals, notched at the top, and supporting horizontal poles.
Walls were made of ocotillo canes, and the roof was covered
with leafy branches. The structure, erected in 1879, was named
the First Presbyterian Church.

A somewhat more sophisticated design was used by the
Anglicans at Millarville, Alberta (bottom). The congregation
reluctantly accepted the unusual manner of construction –
using vertically placed logs – that was suggested by carpenter
Charles Schack. While they agreed to the design in principle,
the parishioners questioned the stability of the structure and
withheld Schack's payment for three months. Their worries
were unfounded; the church has stood its ground firmly for
three-quarters of a century.

Top: the first Presbyterian Church at Phoenix, Arizona. Bottom: Christ
Church, Millarville, Alberta.

152

RUSSIAN JEWS AND UKRAINIANS ON THE PRAIRIES

One group of immigrants from Russia were Jews, who had long been victims of persecution. Jews began to stream out of Russia in 1882. With the help of settlement agencies in England, they found homes in the United States, Canada, South Africa, and other countries.

Some of the first families who arrived in Canada in 1906 were Lithuanians who came by way of Capetown, South Africa. They chose to make a second migration to Canada after reading that the Canadian government was offering free land. On their arrival they joined settlers from other parts of Russia.

One group of immigrants built the House of Israel Synagogue (left), at Edenbridge, Saskatchewan. The synagogue has now closed its doors.

The Ukrainians made up a very large proportion of early immigrants to the Canadian Prairies. From 1896 to 1900, an average of 35,000 Ukrainians crossed the Atlantic each year and established new homes in the Canadian west. St. Michael's Ukrainian Orthodox Church at Gardenton, Manitoba (below and opposite), is the first and one of the most lavishly ornamented of their churches.

Above: The House of Israel Synagogue at Edenbridge, Saskatchewan, built around 1909. Below and opposite: St. Michael's Ukrainian Orthodox Church at Gardenton, Manitoba, completed in 1899. Many ethnic groups from Europe and eastern Canada opened up the Canadian Prairies. The Ukrainians are one of the largest groups there.

CHURCH OF THE ASSUMPTION, MEACHAM, SASKATCHEWAN

The Ukrainians who immigrated to Canada brought with them the strong, vibrant traditions which had flourished through centuries of Russian, Polish, and Austrian domination in the Ukraine. Those who came first arrived in Winnipeg then moved to rural areas. Many settled in Saskatchewan. The Ukrainian Greek Orthodox Church of the Assumption is in keeping with traditional Ukrainian church design which originated in the Byzantine churches of Turkey and Greece. The plan is cross-shaped with each arm of the cross of equal length. There is a large *bani* over the centre and a richly decorated screen called the *ikonostas* below it.

Above: The Ukrainian Greek Orthodox Church of the Assumption of the Holy Virgin Mary was built in 1911 near Meacham, Saskatchewan. Its interior design (opposite) and the decorative elements of the altar (right) show the strong influence of the Greek Orthodox church forms of eastern Europe.

ST. MARY'S MISSION, BITTERROOT VALLEY, MONTANA

For more than three centuries, energetic Jesuit missionaries worked with natives in every corner of North America. The order was suppressed in the second half of the eighteenth century, but they were rehabilitated in 1814. One of the nineteenth-century Jesuit efforts was directed at the Oregon field, the mountains and valleys of the northwest. Father Pierre Jean de Smet was summoned to the mountains by the Flathead Indians, and in 1841 he built St. Mary's Mission in the Bitterroot valley, near today's Stevensville, Montana.

To Chief Big Face of the Flatheads, who had sent for the black-robed Jesuits, the building of the mission was the fulfillment of a prophecy. A few years earlier, a seriously ill teen-aged Flathead girl named Mary had instructed: "Listen to the Black Robes when they come, they have the true prayer; do all they tell you. They are coming and will build the House of Prayer where I am dying." When the mission was built, Chief Big Face exclaimed: "It is the place where little Mary said the House of Prayer would be built!"

Father de Smet went on to build five more missions in the Oregon country. He went over to Europe to raise money and find more missionaries, and one of the recruits who came back was Father Antonio Ravalli. Born in Ferrara, Italy, Ravalli studied medicine, drawing, and mechanics before being ordained in 1843. Two years later he made his first journey to the Bitterroot valley. The Jesuits subsequently closed St. Mary's, but Father Ravalli reopened it in 1866. At that time he erected the present mision (above) out of logs from the abandoned 1841 structures.

Father Ravalli administered to the natives' bodies as well as their souls. Next to the church is a small pharmacy – the first in Montana – where he prepared and administered his medicines. Father Ravalli died in 1884 at the age of 72, and was buried in the cemetery behind the mission church.

Opposite: interior and exterior views of St. Mary's Ukrainian Greek Catholic Church at Dobro Wody, Saskatchewan. Above: the interior of St. Mary's Mission, Bitterroot valley, Montana, built in 1866. It was one of several missions operated by Jesuits in the area. The rather ornate interior belies the fact that it is a simple log structure.

WESTERN MISSIONS

On both sides of the border, Catholic missions played an important part in opening up the west. Originally built to minister to the needs of the Indian population, their presence and their achievements encouraged pioneers to continue moving further westward. St. Mary's Mission in Montana (above) was established by Jesuits. Father Charles John Felix Adolph Marie Pandosy of the Missionary Oblates of Mary Immaculate founded the Okanagan Mission in British Columbia in 1859 (left and opposite). Such missions often included a school, a shop, a mill, and other amenities.

Above: St. Mary's Mission in the Bitterroot valley of Montana (1866), although enhanced by a clapboard façade and a graceful bell tower, has deceptively primitive log construction. The first missionary to serve the Flathead Indians in this region was Father Pierre Jean de Smet, a Belgian Jesuit who founded the original mission in 1841. Left and opposite: Father Charles Pandosy's Okanagan mission near Kelowna, BC, is made of uncovered logs.

ST. SAVIOUR'S ANGLICAN CHURCH, BARKERVILLE, B.C.

Billy Barker was a Cornish sailor of about forty who jumped ship when he heard tales of the gold in British Columbia. Barker went to Richfield, and then a short distance down the canyon of Williams Creek, where he began to dig, much to the amusement of others, who believed that gold was to be found only in surface water. But Billy was right. On August 21, 1862, at the depth of fifty-two feet, he made British Columbia's richest gold strike.

Barkerville, as the instant town around Billy's claim became known, attracted 10,000 persons within a year. Soon it bragged of being the largest city west of Chicago and north of San Francisco. On September 16, 1868, a miner apparently leaned over to kiss a woman at the back of a saloon and knocked over a stovepipe. Within an hour and a half Barkerville had burned to the ground. Fire, of course, was the great risk in every crowded timber mining town. Barkerville was rebuilt at once, but its heyday had passed. Many people chose to go elsewhere, and Barkerville gradually faded into the oblivion of yet another ghost town.

In 1869 the *Cariboo Sentinel*, Barkerville's twice-weekly newspaper, watched St. Saviour's Church (above and opposite) being built, and explained the reason for its steep gable and pointed arched windows:

> The style is "Early English" in which architectural effect is attained by due proportion of parts, bold and simple forms, rather than by elaborate ornament. . . . We congratulate the friends of the Anglican Church on possessing a church so appropriate to their worship. Certainly those who wish to pray, as their fathers prayed, may do so here, in a church which in form, if not in material, will remind them of the village churches of the "fatherland."

As for Billy Barker, after he staked his claim he fetched a bride and returned north. It is said that gold worth $600,000 came out of Barker's shaft. He spent the money as quickly as he earned it. What didn't pass over the bar was given away, loaned, or badly invested, and Billy Barker died penniless in an old folks' home in Victoria in 1894.

Prairies and Plains

"I stretched the Constitution until it cracked," admitted President Thomas Jefferson to Congress in 1803, after strenuous negotiation with France, "yet the fertility of the country, its climate and extent, all promise in due season important aids to our treasury." And thus the Louisiana Purchase, about one million acres west of the Mississippi River, tripled the land area of the young country, formed all or part of thirteen future states, and gave the country its best agricultural land – as well as land believed to be its worst. Attracted by what seemed to be an endless supply of rich unclaimed land, and forced westward by hard times, farmers poured across the Mississippi into the regions that were to become the states of Louisiana, Arkansas, and Missouri.

Missouri grew to be the largest and most prosperous of the three. At the time of the Louisiana Purchase the region was sparsely populated with French villages. The first Americans who joined the French residents came from Kentucky, Tennessee, Virginia, and the southeast. Most of them arrived between 1815 and 1819, when some thirty to fifty wagons filled with impatient farmers and their families crossed the Mississippi at St. Louis every day. The eager homesteaders would rush to a spot along the river valley or up the Missouri River and there stake their claim.

At Chesterfield, a town on the Missouri River some twenty miles west of St. Louis, a group of early pioneers established the first Presbyterian congregation west of the Mississippi. In 1815 they erected their first church – likely of logs; about twenty-five years later they replaced it with an austere grey stone building known today as the Old Bonhomme Church. Its simple lines – simple almost to the point of dullness – reflect the same Presbyterian denial of frills that characterized the denomination's earlier log meeting houses.

Just as the builders of the Old Bonhomme Church brought the simple Presbyterian manner to Missouri, so a group of Episcopalians from Albemarle County in Virginia settled at Eolia, Missouri, and built their version of a Virginia church. The congregation at Eolia (some fifty miles north of Chesterfield) was organized in 1846, and ten years later they erected a church dedicated to St. John. Parishioner John Winn Davis donated the land for the church, as well as its bricks. The small gabled building is three bays long with the main entrance at one end. Superficially, it bears some relationship to the Old Bonhomme Church at Chesterfield. Yet its proportions, the slope of its roof, and the use of brick as the main building material all mark it unmistakably as a descendant of a Virginia church of the colonial period.

The Virginia prototype has, however, been "modernized" to keep up with the current stylistic revivals. There are elements of both the Greek Revival and the Gothic Revival: the pediment atop the façade has the shape and the mouldings of a good Grecian prototype; the pointed windows with curved tracery in the upper part are Gothic in inspiration. The double-hung sashes belong to no particular historical style, but have a sound Virginia pedigree.

Missouri became home to many Europeans–mostly Germans – as well as to eastern Americans. German Lutherans led by Pastor G. H. Loeber erected a two-storey log parsonage in Altenburg in 1839, and services of the newly organized Trinity Lutheran Church were held upstairs. A proper church was erected in 1845; the present Trinity Lutheran Church, the third, rose in 1867. It is a rather conventional rectangular stone structure with a tall steeple over the entrance. One looks in vain for European features. Within thirty years the congregation had become quite Americanized.

As Missouri, Arkansas, and Louisiana filled with settlers, the westward-migrating pioneers sought open space elsewhere. Although they were blocked in the southwest by Indian Territory, the fertile land just to the north (comprising the eastern parts of Iowa and Wisconsin) was opened to white settlement on the first day of June, 1833. Eager pioneers from the adjacent states lined up along the Mississippi, waiting for the signal to cross. "The roads," wrote one newcomer, "were literally lined with the long blue waggons of the emigrants wending their way over the broad prairies."

Near the town of Nashua, Iowa, stands the First Congregational Church of Bradford, better known as "The Little Brown Church in the Vale." Its fame comes from *The Church in the Wildwood*, the song written by music teacher Dr. William S. Pitts:

> Come to the church in the wildwood,
> Oh, come to the church in the vale;
> No spot is so dear to my childhood
> As the little brown church in the vale.

Inspired by the lovely treed site that had been reserved for the church, Pitts composed his verses about a little brown church – only to return a few years later and find such a building standing there. (Its hue is said to have been chosen for want of money to buy more colourful paint.)

The original congregation, organized in 1855, was composed mainly of farmers from New England. The first members worshipped in a log house, a lawyer's office, a hotel dining room, a school house, and an abandoned store. The church was begun a few years later under the direction – and probably to the design – of the Reverend John K. Nutting. The young minister would not be discouraged by the lack of funds or by the interruption caused by the Civil War.

The church, completed in 1864, is every bit as charming as the song suggests. The pointed arched door and windows follow the Gothic Revival, a style by now acceptable to every

Fee Fee Baptist Church near St. Louis, Missouri, was erected in 1827.

The first services of Trinity Church, Altenburg, Missouri, were held in the parsonage (above, left). The present church (above, right) was built in 1867.

denomination. Inside the church a solitary pulpit occupies the central spot as it had in the old Congregational meeting houses of New England – a spot that would be taken up by the altar in an Episcopalian building.

Less than a hundred miles west of the headwaters of the Mississippi River, along the western edge of Minnesota, flows the Red River, whose waters empty into Lake Winnipeg and eventually discharge into Hudson Bay. Because it connects with the Great Lakes to the east and the extensive river system of the Canadian Prairies to the west, the Red River became the hub of the northwestern fur trade.

The first agricultural settlement in the Red River valley came about early in the nineteenth century through the efforts of the Scottish philanthropist-businessman, Thomas Douglas, fifth Earl of Selkirk. He had decided to find New World homes for the poor crofters of Scotland and Ireland who were being driven off the land. One of his settlements was on a large tract of land in the Winnipeg basin. The first settlers there sailed from Scotland to Hudson Bay in 1811 and made the journey to the Red River the next summer. They named their settlement Kildonan, after the Scottish parish from which many of them had come. They faced extreme hardships, not the least of which in their minds was the lack of a clergyman of their own Presbyterian faith – for whom they had to wait forty years.

The first church building to appear in the Red River settlement was that of Father J. N. Provencher's Roman Catholic mission at St. Boniface, erected in 1818 to serve the Métis, the Indians, some French-Canadian settlers, and a group of German-Swiss mercenaries who had come in search of a home. The first British cleric was an Anglican missionary named John West, who had been sent for by the Hudson's Bay Company. In 1823 he built the mission church of St. John's, a log building with a somewhat incongruous steeple that West called "a landmark of Christianity in this wild waste of heathenism." The Church of England service was modified to accommodate the Presbyterians. The two groups lived and prayed side by side in relative harmony.

The most handsome Anglican church to spring up along the river was the church of St. Andrew's built between 1845 and 1849 by the Reverend William Cockran. His congregation was poor, but gave what money, materials, and labour they could so that they might replace their first wooden church with a fittingly impressive limestone structure. Pointed arches over the windows and in the wooden superstructure of the stalwart tower allude to the Gothic Revival. In other respects St. Andrew's has no historical style – its form implicitly recalls the English parish church tradition in the same way as did the Old Brick Church in Virginia some two centuries earlier.

Twenty miles to the southwest, on the shore of the Assiniboine River, the Anglican church of St. James was completed shortly after 1850. It was built in the "Red River frame" method of log construction (as had been St. John's) typical of Manitoba. The logs have been covered on the exterior with sawn wood siding, but the interior reveals the structure clearly. The logs – which had been felled upriver and floated to the site – were hewn square and laid on top of each other. Their ends were shaped with projecting tongues and inserted into grooves cut down the sides of posts, which had first been set upright at intervals upon a sill. This construction method was French in origin; the fur traders had brought it to Manitoba from Quebec. The Anglican churches of the Red River valley reflected the Anglican tradition in their form, but in construction they succumbed to the manners of their neighbours: St. James' was built in the log system that had originated with the French; St. Andrew's in a stone manner characteristic of Scottish masons.

The Scots Presbyterians finally greeted their long-awaited minister in 1851. The Reverend John Black arrived from Montreal in September of that year; in one day 300 Presbyterians abandoned the English church to join his flock. Two years later they completed the Old Kildonan Church, a stone building not unlike St. Andrews. The walls, unfortunately, have since been stuccoed over, destroying the original handsome demeanor.

In the middle years of the nineteenth century the American Great Plains were considered a mere wasteland whose only purpose was to serve as a pathway from east to west. Just as cattlemen were developing their great ranches on the Plains in the 1860s, hordes of farmers began to arrive, threatening their enterprise. The farmers were lured by the Homestead Acts of 1862 and 1866 that promised 160 acres of land free to anyone who would work it for five years. In addition to the arrival of the railroad, a rash of recent technological inventions had made Plains farming feasible. Easterners and Europeans – some as political or religious refugees, others simply lured by the promise of free land – arrived by the tens of thousands. Nebraska and Kansas were opened for settlement in 1854. The Dakotas and the northern Plains states began to be occupied in the 1860s, and the southern states – most notably Oklahoma – two decades later.

The pioneers developed new methods of building as well as of farming. Trees were scarce, for few areas were forested. Lacking lumber, farmers from Saskatchewan to Kansas built their houses out of the material that was most plentiful: the sod that they removed when ploughing their fields. Some of the first pioneer churches were built the same way. Treeless Custer County in central Nebraska had numerous sod churches. They, like the sod houses, have long since disappeared.

Sod was used together with another plentiful material, hay, in the first church for white settlers in Kansas, Plymouth Congregational church in Lawrence. The pioneers, latter-day Puritans from New England, built their church in 1854, the first year of settlement in this portion of former Indian Territory. Two sixty-foot rows of poles inserted into the ground about twenty feet apart were pulled together at the top and tied to a ridge pole. The sloping sides were thatched with hay, and the triangular walls at each end were made of sod with wooden door openings. The church was remarkably similar to the cruck-framed church built by the pioneers' forebears some 250 years earlier in Jamestown. In 1857 the hay-and-sod church was replaced by one of native limestone. In that same year the Methodists and Unitarians built churches in Lawrence, and the Episcopalians followed a year later.

The denominations competed aggressively in the west, hoping perhaps that religion might bring about the stability and order that the law was unable to provide. More often than not the Methodists arrived on the scene first. Reverend William H. Goode of the Northern Indiana Conference was appointed to Kansas only nine days after the territory was opened, and he arrived there a month later. The Methodist circuit-riders had much longer distances to travel in the Plains than had their predecessors in Ontario; when they reached their distant destinations, more often than not they found themselves among settlers who cared little for religion. It was then said of Kansas that "there is no Sunday west of Junction City and no God west of Sabina."

In the early years of settlement few churches were erected beyond the larger towns. The first services were often held out of doors or in tents, schools, or hotels. The First Baptist Church of Big Springs, South Dakota, was organized in a sod stable, while the first sermon in Yankton, in the same state, was preached in a store.

The first missionary to reach the Canadian territory now known as Alberta was a Methodist who arrived in 1840. The Reverend George McDougall was appointed superintendent of Methodist missionary work in the entire Canadian west in 1860, to be joined twelve years later by his son, John. One of the missions they built was for the Mountain Stoney Indians on a magnificent site just west of Calgary, at the foot of the Rocky Mountains. The mission buildings at Morleyville (now simply Morley) – named after the McDougalls' colleague the Reverend W. Morley Punshon–were begun by John in 1873, and a proper church was started two years later. Father George visited in the winter of 1875-1876 and died nearby on a cold January night while returning from a buffalo hunt.

The church, known today as McDougall Memorial United Church, is a simple wood-framed structure, built with materials

The brown First Congregational Church of Bradford, Iowa, was built almost entirely of donated materials and with voluntary labour.

brought from Fort Benton in Montana. A drawing of the late 1870s shows it with no tower. In this original form the structure would hardly have differed from a plain Methodist meeting house of seventy or one hundred years earlier. Only the pointed windows were a concession to church forms. The addition of the spindly tower continued the evolution from meeting house to church.

The missionaries were followed by pioneer farmers. Settlers reached the Canadian Prairies in the 1880s – a few decades later than settlement of the American Plains – after the Canadian government gained title to the land from the Hudson's Bay Company. Churches quickly sprang up everywhere.

A charming church with an unusual method of construction is Christ Church in Millarville, Alberta, not far from Morley. The Reverend R. Murray Webb Peploe settled near Millarville in 1894 and held Anglican services in his home. A year later the area residents decided to build a church. Reverend Webb Peploe donated five acres of land and parishioners gave materials. German-born carpenter Charles Schack and his assistant Frank Watt were the only tradesmen to receive pay.

Although the neighbourhood had a number of sawmills, Webb Peploe and Schack convinced the congregation to use logs taken from a nearby bush and set vertically – a most uncommon method which had been used by Schack for Webb Peploe's own house. Schack admitted that he knew of no other building with vertical logs, nor had he ever built a log structure before. He had devised the method for Webb Peploe's house to minimize shrinkage of the logs so that the walls could be properly plastered. (Other Alberta pioneers occasionally used vertical logs when the available wood was not long or straight enough to lay horizontally.)

The finished building is reminiscent of the palisaded structures built centuries earlier by French pioneers. The logs were put into place, bark and all, but hungry insects worked their way under the bark, which had to be removed. Inside the

Top: St. James' Church, Winnipeg, Manitoba. Bottom: Christ Church in Millarville, Alberta, was built with vertical logs.

church, roof trusses rest on posts that are reinforced by buttress-like logs outside, keeping unnecessary weight off the walls. The system was novel and effective.

Faced with an environment that lacked building traditions, pioneers often improvised in this way. Once they had an idea of how their church should look, they adapted their concept and methods to the materials at hand and were likely to try almost anything. With the rapid growth of the west, however, mass production was sometimes considered a more appropriate measure. The Anglican church began to build on a large scale when, shortly after 1900, it decided to establish a church in every centre of population in mushrooming Saskatchewan. Archdeacon George Exton Lloyd went to England to recruit dozens of young laymen – known as Lloyd's lambs – to assist the overworked clergy.

To keep up with the growth, Lloyd's new churches were built cheaply and quickly to a standardized design. Plans and specifications were carefully worked out so that any local carpenter could assemble the buildings easily from fixed quantities of standard supplies. The designer may have been the Reverend D. T. Davies of Saskatoon, a skilled carpenter. The churches – presumptuously called 'Canterbury Cathedrals" – squeezed sixty worshippers into a nave sixteen feet by twenty feet. A contemporary description noted that they "are to be thoroughly ecclesiastical in design, with tower, Gothic windows and high-pitched roof . . . The tower, which costs about $15, serves as storm-porch in bad weather, conceals the chimney, and serves as the hall-mark of the Church of England throughout the Diocese of Saskatchewan."

Similar caricatures of English churches satisfied North American Anglicans from the seventeenth century to the twentieth. A number of Canterbury Cathedrals survive, but because flexibility was a built-in feature, almost all of them have been drastically altered over the years.

Builders sometimes resorted to fully prefabricated structures as well. Wooden prefabs were common in the Prairies, but apparently not for churches. An iron church, prefabricated in England, was assembled at Churchill on Hudson Bay; another was put together in Victoria, British Columbia.

On the Prairies and Plains, a number of churches were built to serve planned settlements rather than to serve a congregation that simply accumulated in an area. Many western towns began as "colonies" for Europeans of many nations and religions seeking land in the New World. Some were promoted by idealistic, philanthropic colony-planters; others by the aggressive commercialism of the railroads; while still others were developed more casually by immigrants seeking to settle near their countrymen. Cannington Manor in Saskatchewan (mentioned in the Introduction) was one such settlement.

Large numbers of Scandinavians poured onto the Plains on both sides of the border. The 1870s saw the beginning of a mass migration from Iceland that saw 30,000 people – one-third the entire population – come to North America in thirty years. The Reverend Pall Thorlaksson and his flock put down roots at Gardar, North Dakota, near Pembina, where the former fishermen became farmers. Lutheran by faith, they followed the Norwegian Synod – other settlements chose to go in with the Germans – until 1885, when the Icelandic Lutheran Synod was

Many of the first religious services on the Plains took place at camp meetings such as this one (right). From an 1838 lithograph of a painting by Joseph Smith.

St. Joseph's Church was built by German Catholics from Russia.

A woodcarving at St. Michael's Ukrainian Orthodox Church in Gardenton.

organized. Two years later the townsfolk built their first church, a handsome wood frame structure with a tall steeple. The interior is particularly beautiful, with its elegant free-standing wood pulpit resplendent in its carving and crowned by a delicate canopy. A spiky reredos behind the altar perpetuates Gothic Revival imagery. A gilded communion rail defines the sacred area.

A number of oppressed minority groups – many of German origin – left Russia and came to Canada, among them Mennonites, Roman Catholics, Jews, and Ukrainians. The Canadian government had passed the Dominion Land Act in 1872, offering 160 free acres to farmers. Eager to find settlers, the government had sent Wilhelm Hespeler, a German-born immigration agent, to Russia to try to convince German-speaking Mennonites to come to Canada. Delegates visited Canada as guests of the Department of Agriculture and selected land in the Red River valley. Eight townships were reserved, and the Mennonites were guaranteed cheap passage, free land, their own schools, and exemption from military service and oaths.

The Mennonites began to come to Manitoba in 1874. A typical church stands at the Mennonite Village Museum at Steinbach, Manitoba. Built in 1881 to serve the Old Colony Mennonites near Winkler, it was moved to the museum a few

years ago. The church is a plain structure that hardly looks different from a house, just like the Mennonite meeting houses in Pennsylvania a century earlier. Men and women are separated by an aisle. Song leaders, assistant ministers, and deacons sit on a platform beside the pulpit.

The Canadian government was assisted in its promotion of Prairie land by the Canadian Pacific Railway, in an effort to sell its enormous land holdings and to develop traffic. One settlement assisted by the railway was St. Joseph's Colony, a small group of German Catholics from Russia who settled at Balgonie, near Regina, Saskatchewan. The immigrants were mostly from Josephstal, near Odessa. Seeking new homes because of persecution, the first contingent – four families – arrived in 1886 after a three-week trip. They built a small church of mud and stone in 1887. A permanent church was erected ten years later under the guidance of Father J. E. Zerbach. The small community raised money for the ambitious building by canvassing the neighbourhood – even raising $29.25 from their former village of Josephstal in Russia. Contractor S. A. Clark (perhaps also the designer) built the walls of stone to the height of six feet, and placed a lumber superstructure above it. The nave walls and bell tower are opened with round (rather than the customary pointed) arches – possibly a kind of Romanesque revival, reflecting the dominant tradition of Germany.

St. Michael's in Gardenton, Manitoba, was the first Orthodox church in Canada. It was also one of the most elaborate Ukrainian pioneer churches.

Russian Jews known as Ashkenazim – as distinct from the Sephardim from Spain and Portugal who had settled earlier along the east coast – began escaping from Russian persecution in large numbers in the 1880s. One of the most charming little synagogues left to us from this period was built by a Jewish farm community at Edenbridge, Saskatchewan, a wooded area along the Carrot River, which was first settled in 1906. The community remained nameless until it was granted a post office and a name had to be chosen. After a hasty retreat to an English gazetteer the residents settled upon Edenbridge – an Anglicized combination of *Yidden* – Yiddish for "Jews" – and "bridge."

In 1908 or 1909 the House of Israel Synagogue was built near the Carrot River bridge. The tiny building was about the same size as a budget-priced Canterbury Cathedral, but differed in its total avoidance of those features that identified an Anglican structure as a church: it had no tower or pointed windows, and the pitch of the roof was softened by a second ridge at the top. The round-headed windows at the east end – behind the cantor's desk and the ark – may have been intended to evoke historical associations that were vaguely Romanesque (as at St. Joseph's Colony) or even more vaguely Spanish (a common idiom for synagogues).

In many ways the surrounding region is typical of Prairie districts because it is a home to many pioneer ethnic groups.

Some came from England and Ontario and worshipped at St. James Norwood Anglican Church, one of Lloyd's Canterbury Cathedrals. Beside them lived Scandinavians who arrived from Wisconsin and Minnesota and built the Beaver Creek Lutheran Church out of logs. Their neighbours in turn were Slavs from Poland and the Ukraine who erected churches of the Roman Catholic, Greek Catholic, Greek Orthodox, and Russian Orthodox faiths.

The Ukrainians made up a very large proportion of early immigrants to the Canadian Prairies, beginning in 1896. In the previous year the Department of the Interior in Ottawa had received an eloquent letter explaining that many Ukrainian farmers "desire to quit their native country, due to over-population, subdivision of land holdings, heavy taxation, and unfavourable political conditions." The writer, Dr. Josef Oleskow, a Professor of Agriculture and an influential leader of the Ukrainian peasantry, successfully negotiated for land, financial aid, and travel assistance on behalf of his compatriots. In the years that followed, large Ukrainian settlements populated first Manitoba, then Saskatchewan and Alberta.

St. Michael's Ukrainian Orthodox Church in Gardenton, Manitoba, the first Orthodox church in Canada, was built in 1896-1899. The building is wholly unlike other western churches. With its large central domed space – called a *bani* –

Holy Ascension Russian Greek Orthodox Church near Sturgis, Saskatchewan (top and bottom), was built by a poor congregation.

covered by a little onion-shaped cupola, and with its smaller onion domes front and back, St. Michael's has the elaborate silhouette of a church in the settlers' homeland. The cruciform plan with its broad transepts is likewise characteristic of Orthodox churches. The interior is lavishly ornamented.

Not all Ukrainian churches were so elaborate. Holy Ascension Russian Greek Orthodox Church near Sturgis, Saskatchewan, was built in 1905. The rapidly decaying structure – abandoned in 1968 – is built of rough round logs, unfinished with plaster or paint inside or out. (The ends of the logs are "saddle-notched," with their ends projecting beyond the corners, not carefully dovetailed as in more painstakingly constructed log buildings.) The floor is dirt. The steep, shingled roof with its deep overhanging eaves has the profile of the house of a typical Ukrainian pioneer, much like a peasant's cottage in eastern Europe. A home might have been plastered with mud or stucco, its roof thatched rather than shingled, but the appearance was much the same. Some significant differences from houses, however, are seen in the east end, made polygonal to accommodate the Orthodox sanctuary; in the windows, which are overlaid with a few boards to give a pointed illusion; and spiky crosses that rise from the roof.

Just as the Holy Ascension Church is based on the form of the traditional house, the Ukrainian Greek Orthodox Church of the Assumption of the Holy Virgin Mary, near Meacham, Saskatchewan, derives from the traditional Greek Orthodox church form of eastern Europe. Pioneer P. Bodnarchuk donated the land for the church and in 1911 the three Hanrevich brothers built it – and perhaps designed it. The church is made of commercial lumber, with siding covering its frame. Ukrainian Catholic and Orthodox Christians originally attended this church together and were ministered to by a priest supplied by the Russian Orthodox Mission.

One of the most impressive early Ukrainian churches is St. Mary's Ukrainian Greek Catholic Church at Dobro Wody, Saskatchewan. The building is dominated by a magnificent *bani*, roofed in shiny textured tin. Its onion shape immediately identifies the church's Eastern roots. The church is shaped rather like an elongated cross, with an extra room tucked into the rear corner. Its richly decorated interior has hand-painted ornamentation on the walls and a fine *ikonostas* ["screen"] – usually absent in a Catholic church.

Canadian Prairie churches, perhaps more so than those of the Plains to the south, are probably the best reminders of the diverse backgrounds which mingled there in pioneer days. Each national group designed its house of worship according to the forms it had grown up with in its homeland, this time with little ecclesiastical or secular interference. Changes occurred in order to adapt to the materials and technology that were available, or because funds and labour were limited. The changes tended to simplify forms to a kind of folk manner common to all pioneers, but the national origin almost inevitably shows through. George Woodcock has described this persistence of tradition in *Canada and the Canadians*:

> Pioneers are people whose creativity goes into the reshaping of the land. They have neither the time nor the energy to turn their minds to original thought or artistic creation, and they are usually so engrossed in the idea of reproducing in a strange land the world from which they came that the thought of giving a novel expression to what they see is remote from their minds.

A Doukhobor Prayer House in Veregin, Saskatchewan (1917). Over seven thousand Doukhobors emigrated to Canada from Russia in 1899.

THREE BRITISH COLUMBIA CHURCHES

The little church near Vernon, BC (opposite), was built for private worship in 1887. It never had a resident priest; services were conducted by travelling Oblate missionaries. In this respect St. Ann's served in much the same way as a chapel of early Quebec. It even looks rather like one.

The Murray United Church in Nicola, BC (above, left), was built in 1876 for the first Presbyterian congregation to be organized in the British Columbia interior. It was named after its minister, the Scottish Reverend George Murray.

The infamous Stolen Church at Windermere in the Selkirk Mountains of British Columbia (above, right) began its life in 1887 as St. Peter's Anglican Church of Donald, British Columbia, a divisional headquarters of the Canadian Pacific Railway. According to a popular legend, when the line moved the facilities westward to Revelstoke in 1899, the church was ordered moved to that town by rail. Angry parishioners allegedly dismantled the building themselves, loaded it onto an eastbound train, transferred it at Golden to a river barge, and set it up in the town of Windermere at the headwaters of the Columbia River. The 600-pound bell, however, was stolen by the manager of the barge company. It hangs today in St. Paul's at Golden.

Opposite: St. Ann's Church, O'Keefe Ranch, near Vernon, BC. Above, left: Murray United Church at Nicola, BC. Above, right: the Stolen Church, Windermere, BC.

From Sea to Shining Sea

The Pacific Ocean had always been the goal of North American explorers, colonists, and settlers. The founding charter of the Massachusetts Bay Company had granted it title to a strip of land "from the Atlantic Ocean to the South Sea." Succeeding generations of explorers and fur traders searched endlessly for a water route westward to the sea. It was not too long after the birth of the new American nation that its politicians were speaking of Manifest Destiny. The goal was finally realized by Canada and the United States in the middle of the nineteenth century, but not before other nations had attempted to gain control of the Pacific shore.

The assault upon the west coast began simultaneously from the south and from the north. The Spanish began their thrust into California in 1769 with the founding of the first of the Franciscan missions. They were supported by a Spanish colonial government concerned over advances from the north by fur traders from Russia. Merchant Grigorii Ivanovich Shelikhov and his successors were at that time organizing the Russian American Company with posts from Alaska to California. In 1812 the *promyshlenniki* ["fur traders"] built Fort Ross – a name derived from the Spanish *Fuerto de los Rusos* – some seventy miles north of San Francisco. The settlement contained a domed Russian Orthodox chapel of redwood logs, which was destroyed by fire in 1971.

The short-lived Russian presence is best remembered in Alaska, where even today some people speak Russian as a first language. Kenai, south of Anchorage, had first been visited by Russian Orthodox missionaries in 1795. There stands the little Russian Orthodox chapel of St. Nicholas, built some time between 1883 and 1894. The Kenai chapel is a square log building, with cross-gabled roofs and a pyramidal *bani* topped by an onion-domed cupola. It resembles Orthodox churches built on the Canadian Prairies by settlers from eastern Europe who arrived from the opposite direction.

During the eighteenth century the British and Spanish navies made numerous competitive voyages of exploration along the northern Pacific coast, as did New Englanders, but they established few posts. The Spaniards apparently did build a church as far north as Nootka, British Columbia, in 1789, but the settlement never led to anything more than a diplomatic squabble. More permanent settlements came about through the work of the Montreal-based North West Company, Simon Fraser, the Hudson's Bay Company, and Lewis and Clark. The first to follow them were the missionaries.

Four Indians from the Oregon country – three Nez Perces and a Flathead–made the long trip to St. Louis in 1831, allegedly in search of the "white man's Book of Heaven." The press made capital of the visit, and soon the Methodist *Christian Advocate* was receiving contributions from far and wide to send out a missionary. Selected for the duty was the Reverend Jason Lee, a man born in Quebec of New England parents. Lee's party travelled overland and reached the Hudson's Bay Company's Fort Vancouver (now Vancouver, Washington) in early autumn of 1834. He soon established a mission in the valley of the Willamette River, a short distance above the present city of Portland – and far from either the Nez Perces or the Flatheads.

The New England pioneer built a New England house: the main mission building was constructed of frame and covered in clapboards, with a lean-to at the back giving a "salt-box" profile.

The few Indians in the neighbourhood were sickly and uninterested in the mission, but Lee did preach to the community of French farmers who had left the service of the Hudson's Bay Company. Lee's mission acted as a magnet to subsequent pioneers from the east. Dr. John McLoughlin, the Hudson's Bay Company's factor at Fort Vancouver, shrewdly recognized "the formation of a colony of the United States Citizens on the banks of the Columbia" to be "the main or fundamental part" of the missionaries' intentions.

The four Indians who had come to St. Louis, it seems, were actually in search of the "Black Robes," Jesuit missionaries whom they had learned about from other tribes. Father Pierre Jean de Smet, a Belgian Jesuit who had been serving in Missouri and Iowa, responded by founding St. Mary's Mission in the valley of the Bitterroot River, near today's Stevensville, Montana, in 1841. St. Mary's was temporarily abandoned when the traders turned the Indians against their priests, but it was reopened in 1866 under the direction of the remarkable Father Antonio Ravalli. One of his first accomplishments there was to build a mill that would both grind grain and saw lumber. Its saw was made by flattening, chiselling, and filing the iron tire of a wagon wheel. The new mission that he erected at St.

The Russian Orthodox Chapel of St. Nicholas, Kenai, Alaska.

Mary's in 1866 was fashioned out of cottonwood logs taken from the 1841 mission buildings a mile away. The logs were dressed square on the sides, notched at the ends, and chinked. Inside, a coved ceiling of sawn lumber covers the nave. Behind a handsome communion rail lies a triple-arched sanctuary, and a small balcony juts out over the entrance. Statues and paintings line the walls.

Ravalli had already erected very different kinds of buildings at two other northwest missions that had been founded by Father de Smet. In 1847 Ravalli had directed the construction of St. Paul's Mission at Kettle Falls, Washington, using the French-inspired *pièce-sur-pièce* – or "Red River frame" – construction that had come to the northwest with the fur traders. Three years later he began work on a new Sacred Heart Mission for the Cœur d'Alene Indians in Idaho, recreating his own idea of an Italian church there in the mountains near Cataldo. The result was a unique example of boomtown baroque: the Italianate façade is nothing but a false front.

The incredible interior of Sacred Heart Mission has a ceiling of wood carved by Brother Huybrechts – Ravalli's only non-native assistant – to simulate stucco ornament. A deep apse has a simulated dome over it, and everywhere the decoration imitates European models as closely as was possible given the limited tools and resources.

Other Catholic orders also worked in the western moun-tains. Father Charles John Felix Adolph Marie Pandosy of the Missionary Oblates of Mary Immaculate founded a mission on the bank of British Columbia's Okanagan Lake in 1859. The mission house, church, and school were built simply of logs, in sharp contrast to Father Ravalli's architectural acrobatics. Father Pandosy's Okanagan Mission, like the Oregon mission of Methodist Jason Lee, attracted white settlers to the fertile farmland in its vicinity.

Many of the western missions played a vital role in the development of the empty western lands. The greatest number of settlers came by wagon train along the famed Oregon Trail. Five pioneer Baptists who reached Tualitan Plains, in the Willamette valley at the end of the trail, joined together in 1844 to form the first congregation of their faith west of the Rocky Mountains. They met weekly in the log cabin of David T. Lenox, a native of New York who had moved to Kentucky, Illinois, and Missouri before coming by wagon train to Oregon. A year later the Reverend Vincent Snelling became their minister, and in 1853 they built the West Union Baptist Church. The lovely little frame building made of hand-hewn cedar has handsomely simple lines that follow the example of earlier Baptist meeting houses. Its low gabled roof and squat tower are products of the Greek Revival, which was just then sweeping the continent.

The members of the Church of Jesus Christ of Latter-Day

A detail of St. Mary's Mission near Stevensville, Montana.

A corner of the triple-arched sanctuary at St. Mary's Mission, Stevensville.

Saints moved west during this period in search of religious freedom. When Joseph Smith and his brother were killed by a raging mob in Carthage, Illinois, the time had come for the Mormons to push on. For a year their new leader, Brigham Young, led 12,000 followers to their Zion in the barren valley of the Great Salt Lake.

At first the settlers worshipped in social halls, but as time passed more specialized buildings were erected. Meeting houses for worship were called "ward chapels." Groups of wards were organized into stakes, and each stake usually had a larger assembly hall called a "tabernacle," used for secular gatherings as well as for Latter-Day Saints worship. Ward chapels and tabernacles – the equivalent of parish churches and cathedrals – had few special liturgical needs; for this reason most were built in the familiar way and resembled the churches of the eastern states from which the pioneers had come. Four magnificent temples were built in Utah to house the sacred ordinances.

The pioneers along the mountain and coastal frontier were a mixed lot: coarse backwoods trappers and urbane coastal merchants, missionaries, farmers, and ranchers. Soon there would be a new element in their midst. In 1846 California declared its independence from Mexico, and a year of war brought the whole southwest into American hands. Five days after Congress ratified the treaty with Mexico in March, 1848, a small notice on the last page of the San Francisco *Californian* announced that gold had been discovered by men who were building a sawmill near Sacramento. The gold rush was about to begin. The forty-niners rushed to California from all over the United States and staked their claims in the many hills. More gold was discovered in 1858 in British Columbia and in Colorado, and gold and silver were both found in Nevada. Hard on the heels of the prospectors flocked the permanent settlers who provided the necessary commercial and professional services. And with the settlers came the preachers.

Neither houses nor churches could be erected quickly enough to accommodate the hordes of newcomers. In *California's Architectural Frontier*, Harold Kirker describes the "era of worship under canvas": "The Baptists of San Francisco met beneath a roof made from old ships' sails [just like the first Jamestown settlers 250 years earlier], and the Presbyterians crowded into a tent formerly used as the marquee of a Massachusetts military company." The Reverend James Woods preached his first sermon in Stockton "in a tattered tent."

After the tents came the age of prefabricated buildings, used by almost every denomination in boomtowns throughout the west. These structures were, for the most part, no different

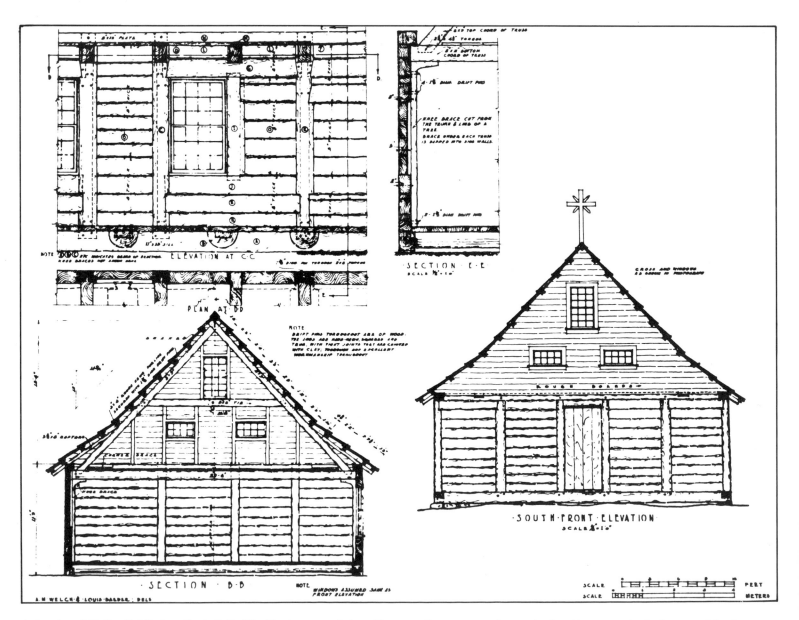

A drawing of St. Paul's Mission, Kettle Falls, Washington, reveals its *pièce-sur-pièce* construction method and its source in the houses of Quebec.

An 1890 photograph of Ravalli's false-fronted Sacred Heart Mission, Cataldo, Idaho. The Tuscan portico is fashioned from six solid logs. The wall timbers are held together with pegs, faced with poles, and covered with mud.

from houses. Many of them were brought from New York by boat around the tip of South America. So too was the galvanized iron used to cover a church of Gothic design on Pine Street in San Francisco: the iron was plastered to imitate stone. And in 1860 the philanthropic Baroness Angela Burdett Coutts of Victoria, British Columbia, ordered iron and steel sections from England, shipped them around the Horn, and had them assembled as St. John's Anglican Church.

After the tents and the prefabs came the permanent churches. As in earlier frontiers, the pioneers recreated the kinds of churches they had known at home in whatever manner the new environment allowed. By the 1850s and 1860s the Gothic Revival had come to dominate American and Canadian church design; this became the standard mode in the new mining towns. Because much of the west coast was a land of dense forest, a new and exciting wood architecture developed.

One of the most alluring yet unassuming of the gold rush churches is St. Saviour's in Barkerville, British Columbia. The town sprang up in 1862 after Cornish sailor Billy Barker struck British Columbia's richest claim — fifty-two feet underground. Barkerville typified the shanty towns of this flamboyant period in western history. Along its main street, which never received a proper name, stood rows of quickly erected frame buildings. A Victoria newspaper described their style as "neither Doric, Ionic, nor Corinthian, but decidedly Columbian." Hotels and saloons sprang up in abundance, and there were all kinds of

stores, breweries, dance halls, houses, a library – and churches.

Anglicans, Catholics, Methodists, and Presbyterians all erected churches in Barkerville or nearby Richfield. St. Saviour's Anglican Church was built in 1869 at the end of the main street furthest from Billy Barker's shaft. The Reverend James Reynard designed it in the hope of providing "a church which shall prove that men working underground have still some hopes which go upward and heavenward."

The church was built in the Gothic Revival style similar to that of Carpenter's Gothic churches of a decade or two earlier, such as St. John Chrysostom in Delafield, Wisconsin. Every significant aspect of St. John Chrysostom has been repeated at Barkerville, but in a simpler form more appropriate to the speed with which the carpenters were forced to work and to the somewhat philistine tastes of the *nouveaux riches* miners. St. John Chrysostom had an uncommon profile much like an A-frame; St. Saviour's was built more conventionally, with higher walls and a steep gable – and made picturesquely asymmetrical with the unselfconscious schoolroom and vestry at the side. The porch has been simplified, and the elaborate bargeboard beneath the eaves has been reduced to saw-cut scallops. The belfry sits in its accustomed position atop the gable. The interior, too, is similar to St. John Chrysostom but less elaborate, and it ends in a curved apsidal chancel with three tall windows. Both churches have vertical board-and-batten siding, a popular framing system in the mining towns because it could be put together easily from standard lumber.

Churches rather similar to St. Saviour's sprang up all over British Columbia. The Anglican church, for one, quickly took firm root in response to the gold rush. The first Anglican service in British Columbia was conducted not by a priest but by a soldier. Colonel R.C. Moody, commander of the Royal Engineers, held a service in the court house at gold-rich Yale in January, 1859. "These Miners' souls," wrote Moody in his diary, ". . . need someone to dwell among them as clergymen." Within a year the colony was organized into a diocese, ministers were becoming plentiful, and churches were under construction up and down the Fraser River. The church of St. John the Divine was dedicated at Yale in 1860. The frame building has the characteristic steep gable with a belfry at its peak. Its façade projects ever so slightly at the centre to give the impression of a full tower.

Wooden churches likewise went up in the mining towns of California, Idaho, and the American northwest. Gold was discovered in Colorado in 1858, and a year later the empty territory acquired its first towns. Denver was one; another was prosperous Central City, Colorado, once called the "richest square mile on earth." The Methodists of Central City immediately organized themselves into a congregation; five years later St. James United Methodist Church began to rise on Eureka Street across from the Assay Office and the Opera House. Semi-arid Colorado lacks the forests of British Columbia, so the church was built of warmly toned local stone. It has much the same steep gable, pointed arches, and slightly projecting tower as had so many wooden churches of the time.

Even after the gold rush era was over, pioneers in the newer areas of the northwest continued to build their churches in the same stripped-down Gothic Revival manner. St. Ann's Roman

Opposite: West Union Baptist Church, Tualitan Plains, Oregon, near the end of the Oregon Trail. It was built in 1853 by the first Baptist congregation west of the Rocky Mountains.

Top: St. James United Methodist Church in Central City, Colorado, a town once called the "richest square mile on earth." Bottom: Our Lady of Tears Church in Silver City, Idaho.

An interior view of the Stolen Church, Windermere, BC, built in 1887.

The interior of St. Ann's Catholic Church near Vernon, BC.

Catholic Church was built in 1887 on the O'Keefe Ranch near Vernon, British Columbia. Cornelius O'Keefe, a native of Ottawa, had in 1867 driven a herd of cattle up from Oregon. He pre-empted a 162-acre tract and eventually expanded it into a 15,000-acre empire.

In its basic form and proportion, as well as in the circular window over the door and in the belfry set back a bit behind the façade, St. Ann's Church is surprisingly similar to parish churches built 150 years earlier in New France. The Gothic Revival door and windows and the pine siding (cut at the ranch's sawmill) make St. Ann's very much a product of its own time and place. But rancher O'Keefe brought to British Columbia the kind of Catholic church with which he would have grown up back east.

Pioneer churches exist even in our own time, combining form from the past with technology of the present. A pioneer church was erected less than a generation ago in Inuvik, a new

Opposite, top: Emmanuel Shearith Chapel, the first church in Denver, Colorado, was built in 1876. It later became Shearith Israel Synagogue. Bottom: This prefabricated iron Anglican church at Churchill, Manitoba, was shipped from England.

town planted one hundred miles north of the Arctic Circle in the Northwest Territories. The government of Canada created Inuvik – Eskimo for "place of man" – in 1954 as an administrative centre for the western Arctic. The Roman Catholic church of Our Lady of Victory was built to serve the new community. To avoid the necessity of melting the permafrost, the church was placed upon pilings driven into holes that were blasted into the tundra by jets of steam. The design concept, however, is as old as the construction technology is new: Our Lady of Victory is a circular church made of white blocks of wood and covered with a bronze dome. The source, of course, is the native igloo built of blocks of snow. Gothic Revival windows identify the structure as an "igloo-church."

Three and one-half centuries ago, a Franciscan friar trekked across the New Mexico desert to inaccessible Acoma and built a mission that combined native building traditions with Spanish conceptions of a church-like appearance. In the middle of our own century, an architect flew over the Arctic to remote Inuvik and designed a house of worship that merged native forms with European-Canadian notions of what a church should look like. The former is one of the oldest churches in North America; the latter one of the newest. Both are pioneer churches.

Our Lady of Victory Roman Catholic Church, Inuvik, Northwest Territories, was built to serve the Arctic community created by the Canadian government in 1954.

Bibliography

The following bibliography includes those studies that have been most helpful in the preparation of this work, as well as those that would be of particular interest to readers who might want to pursue a specific topic. A book or an article that pertains to more than one chapter is cited either with the first chapter to which it is relevant, or else in the preliminary General Studies section. Where a recent book or definitive article contains full references to earlier studies, usually only the newer publication is mentioned.

One periodical and two institutional resources that are cited frequently have been abbreviated:

JSAH   *Journal of the Society of Architectural Historians;*
HABS   Unpublished report, Historic American Buildings Survey, Library of Congress, Washington, DC; and
NHPSB Unpublished report, Research Division, National Historic Parks and Sites Branch, Department of Indian and Northern Affairs, Ottawa, Ontario.

GENERAL STUDIES

A good recent general historical geography of Canada is R. Cole Harris and John Warkentin, *Canada Before Confederation* (New York, 1974). The best history of American settlement is Ray Allen Billington (with James Blaine Hedges), *Westward Expansion: A History of the American Frontier* (4th ed., New York, 1974). The books of Louis B. Wright offer a fine cultural history of the United States; see his *The Cultural Life of the American Colonies 1607-1763* (New York, 1957); *Culture on the Moving Frontier* (Bloomington, Indiana, 1955); and the more popular *Everyday Life on the American Frontier* (New York, 1968).

A general introduction to Canadian religious development may be found in the essays in John Webster Grant, ed., *The Churches and the Canadian Experience* (Toronto, 1963). Sydney E. Ahlstrom has treated American religious history thoroughly in *A Religious History of the American People* (New Haven, 1972). A useful reference work is Frank S. Mead, *Handbook of Denominations in the United States* (4th ed., New York, 1965).

Alan Gowans, *Building Canada: An Architectural History of Canadian Life* (Toronto, 1966), offers an overview of Canadian architecture, as does Douglas S. Richardson, ed., *A Concise History of Canadian Architecture* (Toronto, 1977). A popular guidebook with a surprising amount of good information is the Reader's Digest and Canadian Automobile Association's *Explore Canada* (n.p., 1974). The best guides to the United States are the volumes published since the 1930s by the Federal Writers' Project. Hugh Morrison, *Early American Architecture* (New York, 1952), is still an excellent survey of American colonial building.

Edward F. Rines, *Old Historic Churches of America* (New York, 1936), although old, often inaccurate, and indifferent to architectural history, is the only book to attempt to cover church buildings on a national scope. No such volume exists for Canada, although the United Church of Canada recently issued a series of booklet guides entitled *Church Historic Sites* (4 vols., Toronto, n.d.). A partial list of Canadian churches was obtained from the Canadian Inventory of Historic Building, Department of Indian and Northern Affairs, Ottawa. A succinct study that skilfully relates religious beliefs to church architecture, and whose conclusions are mirrored throughout this book, is Donald Drew Egbert, "Religious Expression in American Architecture," in James Ward Smith and A. Leland Jamison, eds., "Religious Perspectives in American Culture" (Vol. II, *Religion in American Life*, Princeton, 1961), 361-411.

INTRODUCTION

The best description of the Old Brick Church is James Grote Van Derpool, "The Restoration of St. Luke's, Smithfield, Virginia," JSAH (XVII:1, March, 1958), 12-18. Thomas T. Waterman compares it to other churches in Virginia and England in "The Bruton Church of 1683 and Two Contemporaries," JSAH (IV:3-4, July-October, 1944), 43-46. HABS also has useful material.

"The Settlement of Cannington Manor," by Lily Pierce Page, was published in John Hawkes, *The Story of Saskatchewan and its People* (Vol. II, Chicago, 1924). A description of Cannington Manor by Ms. Page's sister, Jessie Pierce Beckton, forms the basis of *All Saints Cannington Manor*, a leaflet by Mrs. A.E.M. Hewlett (Wawota, Sask., n.d.). See also Mrs. Hewlett's *A Saskatchewan Historic Site: Cannington Manor Historic Park* and the Saskatchewan Department of Natural Resources' *Cannington Manor Historic Park* (both n.p., n.d.).

Ernst Kris explains the nature of caricature in *Psychoanalytic Explorations in Art* (New York, 1952). Kris and collaborator E.H. Gombrich further discuss parallels between caricatures and dreams, permitting one to suggest that pioneers relied upon dream-like images of their past in creating new buildings. Richard Krautheimer discusses the associational aspects of architectural "copies" in the Middle Ages in "Introduction to an 'Iconography of Medieval Architecture,' " *Journal of the Warburg and Courtauld Institutes* (V, 1942), 1-33.

Frederick Jackson Turner's "The Significance of the Frontier in American History" was published in American Historical Association, *Annual Report for the Year 1893* (Washington, 1894), 199-227. The best summary of Turner's own views, as well as those of his supporters and critics, may be found in Ray Allen Billington, ed., *The Frontier Thesis: Valid Interpretation of American History?* (New York, 1966). Its relevance to Canada is debated in Michael S. Cross, ed., *The Frontier Thesis and the Canadas* (Toronto, 1970).

The study by Harold Kirker is *California's Architectural Frontier* (1960; Santa Barbara, 1973). John McCoubrey discusses the impact of the environment upon painting in *American Tradition in Painting* (New York, 1963). The interaction between continuity and change in the formation of artistic style is discussed by James Ackerman in "Western Art History," in James Ackerman and Rhys Carpenter, *Art and Archaeology* (Princeton, 1963).

THE FRENCH COLONISTS

The best histories of New France published in English are Marcel Trudel, *The Beginnings of New France 1524-1663*

(Toronto, 1973); W.J. Eccles, *Canada Under Louis XIV 1663-1701* (Toronto, 1964); and Gustave Lanctot, *A History of Canada* (Vol. I, Toronto, 1963). The standard sources are H.P. Biggar, ed., *The Works of Samuel de Champlain* (6 vols., Toronto, 1922); and Marc Lescarbot, *The History of New France*, ed. and trans. by W.L. Grant (3 vols., Toronto, 1907). An early, but still helpful, biography is N.F. Dionne, *Champlain* (London, 1926). See also M. Bishop, *Champlain: The Life of Fortitude* (Toronto, 1963). The standard biography of Laval is H.A. Scott, *Bishop Laval* (London, 1926).

Three classic studies of Quebec churches are [Pierre-Georges Roy,] *Les vieilles églises de la province de Québec* (Quebec, 1925); Ramsey Traquair, *The Old Architecture of Quebec* (Toronto, 1947); and Alan Gowans, *Church Architecture in New France* (Toronto, 1955). For information on the buildings and architects of Quebec City, see A.J.H. Richardson, "Guide to the Architecturally and Historically Most Significant Buildings in the Old City of Quebec . . . ," *Bulletin of the Association for Preservation Technology* (II: 3-4, 1970), 3-144.

The individual churches in the text are all discussed in these general books. The principal monographs are Luc Noppen, *Notre-Dame-des-Victoires à la Place Royale de Québec* (Quebec, 1974); and *The Historical Shrine of Notre Dame des Victoires*, an undated booklet available at the church; Ramsay Traquair and C.M. Barbeau, *The Church of St. Francois [sic] de Sales, Island of Orleans, Que.* (McGill University Publications, XIII: 14, 1926); and the same authors' *The Church of Saint Famille, Island of Orleans, Que.* (No. 13 in the same series). The Ursuline Chapel is discussed in Jean Trudel, *Un chef d'œuvre de l'art ancien du Québec: La chappelle des Ursulines* (Quebec, 1972). The attribution of the tabernacle in the chapel appears in Raymonde Gauthier, *Les tabernacles anciens du Québec des XVIIe, XVIIIe et XIXe siècles* (Quebec, 1974). For Acadian churches, see A.A. Johnstone, *A History of the Catholic Church in Eastern Nova Scotia* (2 vols., Antigonish, 1960).

For the Church of the Holy Family, see Charles E. Peterson, "Notes on Old Cahokia," *French American Review* (I, 1948), 184-225, and HABS notes. Peterson has also written the best statements on French construction in the Mississippi valley: see his "Early Ste. Genevieve and its Architecture," *Missouri Historical Review* (XXXV, 1941), 207-232; and "Colonial Saint Louis," *Bulletin of the Missouri Historical Society* (XXX, 1946-47, and XXXI, 1947-48), *passim*.

The excavations at the Huronia mission are described by Wilfrid Jury and Elsie McLeod Jury, *Sainte-Marie among the Hurons* (Toronto, 1954). A more popular study that offers good illustrations of the reconstructed buildings is John F. Hayes, *Wilderness Mission: The Story of Sainte-Marie among the Hurons* (Toronto, 1969).

THE SPANISH MISSIONARIES

The early explorations and conquests of the Spanish are described in general histories of the United States. The journals of the explorers are collected in Frederick W. Hodge and Theodore H. Lewis, eds., *Spanish Explorers in the Southern United States 1528-1543* (1907; New York, 1965); and Herbert Eugene Bolton, ed., *Spanish Exploration in the Southwest, 1542-1706* (1908; New York, 1963). Stephen Clissold tells the story of *The Seven Cities of Cíbola* (London, 1961). For New Mexico, see especially Russell McKee, *The Last West: A History of the Great Plains of North America* (New York, 1974).

The architectural contributions of the Spanish missionaries and settlers are summarized in Morrison, *Early American Architecture*. Trent Sanford discusses the *Architecture of the Southwest* (New York, 1950). George Kubler, *The Religious Architecture of New Mexico* (1940; Chicago, 1962), is the classic study of that subject. Mission San Estevan at Acoma is described in Mrs. William T. Sedgwick, *Acoma, The Sky City* (Cambridge, Mass., 1926). The best original account of the California misions is Francisco Palóu, *Historical Memoirs of New California*, ed. Herbert E. Bolton (4 vols., Berkeley, 1926). John Berger gives an account of coastal activity in *The Franciscan Missions of California* (New York, 1941). Of Rexford Newcomb's three books on Spanish Californian architecture, most useful is his *Old Mission Churches and Historic Houses of California* (Philadelphia, 1925). The cultural and political impact of the missions is discussed in Herbert E. Bolton, "The Mission as a Frontier Institution in the Spanish-American Colonies," *American Historical Review* (XXIII, 1917-18), 42-61.

THE ENGLISH SETTLERS: THE ANGLICANS AND THE SOUTH

The settlement of the American colonies is treated in depth in two classic studies: Herbert L. Osgood, *The American Colonies in the Seventeenth Century* (3 vols., New York, 1904-07); and Charles M. Andrews, *The Colonial Period of American History* (4 vols., New Haven, 1934-38). Among the more interpretive histories, Thomas Jefferson Wertenbaker, *The First Americans* (New York, 1927), is a useful older volume. Also helpful are Richard B. Morris, *The New World* (New York, 1963); David Hawke, *The Colonial Experience* (Indianapolis, 1966); Wesley Frank Craven, *The Colonies in Transition* (New York, 1968); and Walter D. Edmonds, *The Musket and the Cross* (Boston, 1968).

The most valuable book to treat the church architecture of the original colonies is Harold Wickliffe Rose, *The Colonial Houses of Worship in America* (New York, 1963). Stephen P. Dorsey, *Early English Churches in America 1607-1807* (New York, 1952), is restricted to churches of the Anglican faith.

The buildings of the South are the subject of George Carrington Mason, *Colonial Churches of Tidewater Virginia* (Richmond, 1945); and Henry Chandlee Forman, *The Architecture of the Old South: The Medieval Style 1585-1850* (Cambridge, Mass., 1948). Newer is James S. Rawlings and Vernon Perdue-Davis, *Virginia's Colonial Churches: An Architectural Guide* (Richmond, 1963).

The arrival of the first Virginia settlers is treated well in Thomas Jefferson Wertenbaker, *The Government of Virginia in the Seventeenth Century* (Williamsburg, 1957). For the role of religion in the early settlements, see Perry Miller, "The Religious Impulse in the Founding of Virginia: Religion and Society in Early Literature," *William and Mary Quarterly* (III: 5, 1948), 492-522; and George MacLaren Brydon, *Religious Life in Virginia in the Seventeenth Century* (Williamsburg, 1957). The short-lived Spanish presence there forms the topic of Clifford M. Lewis and Alfred J. Loomie, *The Spanish Jesuit Mission in Virginia 1570-1572* (Chapel Hill, 1953).

Captain John Smith's writings have been collected into his *Works, 1608-1631*, ed. by Edward Arber (2 vols., Birmingham, 1884). Two useful biographies are Bradford Smith, *Captain*

John Smith: His Life and Legend (Philadelphia, 1953); and Philip L. Barbour, The Three Worlds of Captain John Smith (London, 1964).

For early Jamestown, see H.C. Forman, Jamestown and St. Mary's: Buried Cities of Romance (Baltimore, 1938); and John L. Cotter, Archaeological Excavations at Jamestown . . . (Washington, 1958). European cruck-building is discussed in F.W.B. Charles, Medieval Cruck-Building and its Derivatives (London,1967); and newer material appears in F.W.B. Charles and Walter Horn, "The Cruck-Built Barn of Leigh Court, Worcestershire, England," JSAH (XXXII, 1973), 5-29. The second Jamestown church is described in Samuel Purchas, Purchas his Pilgrims (XIX, Glasgow, 1906).

The conservatism of Virginia church design and the continuing use of wood for construction were discussed by Christopher Owens in "Builders, Vestries, Liturgy, and the Creation of the Tidewater Anglican Church Form," a paper read to the Society of Architectural Historians (Boston, 1975). Excerpts from the vestry book of St. Peter's Church are recorded in HABS notes, and the church's history is given in Historic Saint Peter's Protestant Episcopal Church (n.p., n.d.), a booklet formerly distributed at the church.

The relationship of architecture to liturgy is discussed thoroughly by G.W.O. Addleshaw and Frederick Etchells in The Architectural Setting of Anglican Worship (London, 1948). Samuel Chamberlain, Behold Williamsburg (New York, n.d.), tells of the installation of the Liberty Bell in Bruton Parish Church. The architecture of St. James' Church, Goose Creek, is discussed thoroughly by Harley J. McKee in HABS notes.

THE ENGLISH SETTLERS: THE DISSENTERS AND THE NORTH

The Plymouth Company's abortive settlement on the Kennebec, which they called the Sagadahoc, is described best in Andrews, Colonial Period of American History; its church is cited in Forman, Jamestown and St. Mary's. William Bradford's account of the Pilgrims' settlement is taken from William T. Davis, ed., Bradford's History of Plymouth Plantation (1908; New York, 1964); Nathaniel Morton's from New England's Memorial (1669; New York, 1937).

Cotton Mather's remarks are from his Magnalia Christi Americana (London, 1702); his remarks and those by Richard Mather are quoted in Thomas Jefferson Wertenbaker, The Puritan Oligarchy (New York, 1947). For a fascinating account of life in one Massachusetts town, see Sumner Chilton Powell, Puritan Village (Middletown, Conn., 1963).

The New England meeting houses are discussed in the studies cited with Chapter 3, and also in Elise Lathrop, Old New England Churches (Rutland, Vt., 1938); Edmund W. Sinnott, Meetinghouse and Church in Early New England (New York, 1963); and Eva A. Speare, Colonial Meeting-Houses of New Hampshire (n.p., 1938).

John Coolidge gives a full account of the Old Ship Meeting House in "Hingham Builds a Meetinghouse," New England Quarterly (XXXIV, 1961), 435-461. Marian Donnelly, in The New England Meeting Houses of the Seventeenth Century (Middletown, Conn., 1968), gives convincing evidence to show that the meeting house combined aspects of the Anglican church and the secular town hall. Early Dissenters' "chapels" in England are described by Martin S. Briggs in Puritan Architecture (London, 1946). The American offspring of these house-like chapels are the meeting houses of the Quakers and other more radical Protestant denominations (see Chapter 5). Protestant "churches" in Holland and "temples" in France are discussed in Anthony Garvan, "The Protestant Plain Style Before 1630," JSAH (IX:3, October, 1950), 5-13.

The quotation by the Maine developer is from Lathrop, Old New England Churches; that on the centring of the meeting house is from John Winthrop, The Winthrop Papers (Boston, 1929-47), quoted in Donnelly, New England Meeting Houses.

Alan Gowans treats "New England Architecture in Nova Scotia" in Art Quarterly (XXV, 1962), 6-33. The meeting house at Barrington is described in Evelyn M. Richardson, Barrington's Old Meeting Place (n.p., 1968), and in a NHPSB report. The Maugerville settlers are discussed in James Hannay, "The Maugerville Settlement, 1763-1824," Collections of the New Brunswick Historical Society (I, Saint John, 1894); and Frederick Allison McGrand, Backward Glances at Sunbury and Queens (Fredericton, 1967). The history of the Old Covenanters' Church is told in a NHPSB paper. A Visit to Historic Trinity Church in Newport (Newport, 1973), offers an historical guide to that church. Reginald V. Harris, The Church of Saint Paul in Halifax, Nova Scotia: 1749-1949 (Toronto, 1949), is a thorough monograph on that building. The churches at Auburn and Clementsport are touched on in Heritage Trust of Nova Scotia, Seasoned Timbers (I, Halifax, 1972).

THE SETTLEMENT OF THE MIDDLE COLONIES

A fine older study of the social history of the middle colonies that emphasizes architecture is Thomas Jefferson Wertenbaker, The Founding of American Civilization: The Middle Colonies (New York, 1938).

Early Dutch architecture receives quick treatment in R.W.G. Vail, "The Beginnings of Manhattan," JSAH (XI:2, May, 1952), 19-21; and a more thorough accounting is made in Helen W. Reynolds, Dutch Houses in the Hudson Valley Before 1776 (1929; New York, 1965). De Vries' story of the New Amsterdam church is told best in Maud W. Goodwin, Dutch and English on the Hudson (New Haven, 1919). The Fort Herkimer church has been treated by HABS. Christopher Ward, The Dutch and Swedes on the Delaware 1609-64 (Philadelphia, 1930), is the standard study of the two Delaware valley cultures. Israel Acrelius, A History of New Sweden (1759; Ann Arbor, 1966), written by a pastor of the Wilmington church, is a basic source. For his church, see Holy Trinity (Old Swedes) Church: A Photographic Tour (Wilmington, 1974); and Holy Trinity: Old Swedes Church (n.p., n.d.)—two booklets available at the church – and HABS notes. Old Swedes in Philadelphia is also covered by HABS.

Log construction is the subject of Harold Shurtleff, The Log Cabin Myth (Cambridge, Mass., 1939). Henry Glassie has studied log cabins and their European sources; see especially his "The Types of the Southern Mountain Cabin," in Jan Harold Brunvand, The Study of American Folklore (New York, 1968), Appendix C.

The Old Dutch Church in Halifax is the subject of a NHPSB report. Melville N. Cockburn and H. Willa MacCoubrey tell A History of Greenock Church (n.p., 1974). Edward Deming Andrews, in The People Called Shakers (1953; New York, 1963), gives evidence to suggest that the New Lebanon meeting house was originally only two storeys high with a gambrel roof. The New Castle Presbyterian Church has been studied by HABS. For the Newport synagogue, see Carl Bridenbaugh, *Peter Harrison: First American Architect* (Chapel Hill, 1949). Recent research on the Indian Castle Church is summarized in Wayne Lenig, "Archaeology, Education, and the Indian Castle Church" (unpublished manuscript, c. 1973).

EXPANDING THE FRONTIER

For the settlement of Kentucky, Tennessee, and the Northwest Territories, see Emerson Hough, *The Way to the West* (Indianapolis, 1903); John T. Faris, *On the Trail of the Pioneers* (New York, 1920); and Ray Allen Billington, *America's Frontier Settlement* (New York, 1966). Early Ontario history is summarized well in Gerald M. Craig, *Upper Canada: The Formative Years 1784-1841* (Toronto, 1963). A good older history is William Canniff, *History of the Settlement of Upper Canada* (1869; Belleville, 1971). For social history, see the books published a half-century ago by Edwin Guillett; S.D. Clark, *The Social Development of Canada* (Toronto, 1946); the same author's *Church and Sect in Canada* (Toronto, 1948); and G.P. de T. Glazebrook, *Life in Ontario: A Social History* (Toronto 1968). See also J.H. Stewart Reid, K. McNaught, and H.S. Crowe, *A Source Book of Canadian History* (Toronto, 1959).

The architecture of the American regions is treated well in two books by Rexford Newcomb: *Architecture of the Old Northwest Territory* (Chicago, 1950), and *Architecture in Old Kentucky* (Urbana, 1953).

Providence Church is described briefly in *Upper Canada Village: Ontario's Living Heritage* (n.p., n.d.). The statement by Catherine Parr Traill is from *The Backwoods of Canada* (1836; Toronto, 1971). Old Barratt's Chapel is described in HABS. The activities of the Methodists in Ontario are considered in G.F. Playter, *The History of Methodism in Canada* (Toronto, 1862); see also C. Stuart, *The Emigrant's Guide to Upper Canada* (London, 1820). Brock's comment is from a letter cited in Craig, *Upper Canada*.

Most of the Ontario churches are treated in Marion MacRae and Anthony Adamson, *Hallowed Walls: Church Architecture of Upper Canada* (Toronto, 1975). Playter describes the building of the White Chapel, as does *Picton's 100 Years 1837-1937* (Picton, 1937); and W.R. Lunn and Janet Lunn, *The County:The First 100 Years in Loyalist Prince Edward* (Picton, 1967). The history of Williamstown and other settlements is contained in J.G. Harkness, *Stormont, Dundas and Glengarry: A History 1784-1945* (Oshawa, 1946). The architecture of St. Andrew's and the White Chapel is considered in Ralph Greenhill, Ken Macpherson, and Douglas Richardson, *Ontario Towns* (Ottawa, 1974). The history of St. Andrew's West was learned in a series of letters to the author from Mr. Edwin McDonald of that town. St. Raphael's is described in press releases from the Ontario Heritage Foundation (Toronto, c. 1974) in connection with the rededication of the ruins.

The story of the Cathedral of the Holy Trinity in Quebec is told in Frederick C. Würtele, *The English Cathedral of Quebec* (Quebec, c. 1891), and in A.H. Crowfoot, *A Perambulation of the English Cathedral, Quebec* (Quebec, 1947), both of which quote the report submitted by Major Robe. Thomas R. Millman has written the definitive biography of *Jacob Mountain: First Lord Bishop of Quebec* (Toronto, 1947).

St. Stephen's, Chambly, is described by C.P.C. Downman, ed., *History of St. Stephen's Anglican Church, Chambly, Que.* (n.p., 1970); and in the research papers by Peter Noone and Carmen Durand for NHPSB.

St. Joseph's Cathedral, Bardstown – now only a parish church – is discussed in data from HABS. St. Francis Xavier Cathedral, Vincennes, is treated in Curtis G. Shake, *The Old Vincennes Cathedral and its Environs* (Vincennes, 1934); and Henry S. Cauthorn, *A History of the City of Vincennes* (Cleveland, 1902). Information on the Congregational Church, Tallmadge, is found in W.C. Kidney, *Historic Buildings of Ohio* (Pittsburgh, 1972); and I.T. Frary, *Early Homes of Ohio* (Richmond, 1936).

REMEMBRANCE OF THINGS PAST

Much has been written about the phenomenon of Romanticism; besides the general histories of architecture, see the interpretation in James Early, *Romanticism and American Architecture* (New York, 1965). The classic description of the Greek Revival is Talbot Hamlin, *Greek Revival Architecture in America* (1944; New York, 1964). The quotation from Robert Mills is from his manuscript "The Architectural Works of Robert Mills," reprinted in Don Gifford, ed., *The Literature of Architecture* (New York, 1966).

Information on the Second Presbyterian Church in Madison (later St. Paul's Lutheran Church, and now the home of Historic Madison Inc.) and the First (now United) Methodist Church at Taylors Falls mostly came from HABS. St. Andrew's is treated by E.R. Arthur in *St. Andrew's Church, Niagara-on-the-Lake* (Bulletin 153, School of Engineering Research, University of Toronto, Toronto, 1938); and by Peter John Stokes, *Old Niagara-on-the-Lake* (Toronto, 1971).

The most readable discussion of the British origins of the Gothic Revival – and in most respects still the best – is Kenneth Clark, *The Gothic Revival* (2nd ed., London, 1962). The French Gothic Revival has never been properly treated.

St. Mary's Seminary Chapel and its architect have been treated in Robert L. Alexander, *The Architecture of Maximilian Godefroy* (Baltimore, 1974). The best and most recent discussion of Notre Dame is Franklin Toker, *The Church of Notre-Dame in Montreal* (Montreal, 1970). For St. John's in Saint John, see Archibald Lang Fleming, *A Book of Remembrance* (Saint John, 1925). The records of the building committee of Christ Church, Burritt's Rapids, are preserved by the church. The founding of the community is described in Robert Legget, *Rideau Waterway* (2nd ed., Toronto, 1972).

For a comprehensive study of North American ecclesiology, including the histories of Christ Church Cathedral, Fredericton, and St. John Chrysostom, Delafield, see Phoebe Stanton, *The Gothic Revival and American Church Architecture* (Baltimore, 1968). The latter is also discussed in Richard Perrin, *The Architecture of Wisconsin* (Madison, 1967), and in HABS notes. The design by Richard Upjohn is from his *Upjohn's Rural Architecture* (New York, 1852). For the architect, see Everard M. Upjohn, *Richard Upjohn: Architect and Churchman* (New York, 1939). The passage from A.J. Downing is taken from *The Architecture of Country Houses* (1850; New York, 1969).

The Sharon Temple and its worshippers are treated in James L. Hughes, *Sketches of the Sharon Temple and of its founder David Willson* (Toronto, c. 1918); in an article by W.L. Mackenzie written in 1828 and reprinted in J.S. Moir,

The Cross in Canada (Toronto, 1966); and in John Mitchell, The Settlement of York County (County of York, 1950). The Kirtland Temple is discussed in the books by Newcomb, Kidney, and Frary cited in the previous chapter; see also D.S. Andrew and L.B. Blank, "The Four Mormon Temples in Utah," JSAH (XXX, 1971), 51-65; and the notes in HABS.

PRAIRIES AND PLAINS

The story of the discovery and development of the west is told in Frederic L. Paxson, History of the American Frontier, 1763-1893 (Boston, 1924); and McKee, The Last West. The Old Bonhomme Church has been recorded by HABS. St. John's Episcopal Church in Eolia is discussed in Dorothy J. Caldwell, ed., Missouri Historic Sites Catalogue (Columbia, 1963). The history of the Saxon Lutherans of Altenburg is related in the leaflet "Altenburg and the Saxon Lutheran Settlements of East Perry County in Missouri," (n.p., n.d.). M.R. Hinds, The Little Brown Church in Story and in Song (n.p., n.d.), gives the history of that house of worship.

The best histories of Manitoba are Arthur S. Morton, A History of the Canadian West to 1870-71 (2nd. ed., Toronto, 1973); and W.L. Morton, Manitoba: A History (2nd ed., Toronto, 1967). The Red River settlement is discussed there and in numerous other studies, including John West, The Substance of a Journal During a Residence at the Red River Colony (1824; Wakefield, 1966), which illustrates St. John's mission church. St. Andrew's is discussed in NHPSB reports; and in Colin Inkster, "William Cochran," in W.B. Heeney, ed., Leaders of the Canadian Church (Vol. II, Toronto, 1920), 39-61.

The settlement of the American Plains is treated in Everett Dick, The Sod-House Frontier, 1854-1890 (New York, 1938); the settlement of the Canadian Prairies in D. Hill, The Opening of the Canadian West (London, 1967). E.R. DeZurko offers a comprehensive treatment of "Early Kansas Churches," Kansas State College Bulletin (XXXIII:5, April, 1949), 1-68. For the McDougall Church in Morley, see Hugh A. Dempsey, ed., "The Last Letters of Rev. George McDougall," Alberta Historical Review (XV:2, Spring, 1967), 20-25; John McDougall, Opening the Great West: Experiences of a Missionary in 1875-76 (Calgary, 1970); and Ken Liddell, Alberta Revisited (Toronto, 1960). Marsha Snyder presents the history of Christ Church, Millarville, in a NHPSB report; other material is from the church's minute book and parish register, and from a letter from Charles Schack to Eileen Jamieson (1938), all in the Glenbow-Alberta Institute, Calgary. The Canterbury Cathedrals are described in Norman Tucker, Handbook of English Church Expansion (Toronto, 1907); and their history has been reconstructed from W.F. Payton, An Historical Sketch of the Diocese of Saskatchewan of the Anglican Church of Canada (Prince Albert, c. 1973); and from letters to the author from a number of knowledgeable and helpful Saskatchewan clergymen.

Gardar Pioneer Lutheran Church is described in Marilyn Hagerty, "Icelandic Pioneer Church Reaches Ripe Age," Grand Forks Herald (Oct. 24, 1974). The Mennonite settlements are recounted in E.K. Francis, In Search of Utopia: The Mennonites in Manitoba (Altona, 1955); and Mennonite Village Museum: Your Tour Guide (Steinbach, 1974). For the role of the Canadian Pacific Railway, see James B. Hedges,

Building the Canadian West: The Land and the Colonization Policies of the Canadian Pacific Railway (New York, 1939). A. Becker recounts the story of "St. Joseph's Colony, Balgonie," in Saskatchewan History (XX:1, Winter 1967, 1-18). The history of Edenbridge is told in R.M. of Willow Creek No. 458: Jubilee Year 1912-1962 (Melfort, Sask., 1962); S. Jackson, "The Establishment of Edenbridge as a Jewish Farming Community" (unpublished paper, University of British Columbia, 1969); and A.J. Arnold, "The Contribution of the Jews to the Opening and Development of the West," Transactions of the Historical and Scientific Society of Manitoba (III: 25, 1968-69). Ukrainian immigration is the subject of Vladimir J. Kaye, Early Ukrainian Settlements in Canada, 1895-1900 (Toronto, 1964); and Michael H. Marunchak, The Ukrainian Canadians: A History (Winnipeg, 1970). The Ukrainian churches in Saskatchewan have been studied by the Canadian Centre for Folk Culture Studies, in its Church Historical Information Research Project (Ottawa, begun 1971).

FROM SEA TO SHINING SEA

The most useful general histories of the western states and provinces are Dorothy O. Johansen and Charles M. Gates, Empire of the Columbia: A History of the Pacific Northwest (2nd ed., New York, 1967); Oscar Osburn Winther, The Great Northwest: A History (2nd ed., New York, 1964); Ralph J. Roske, Everyman's Eden: A History of California (New York, 1968); and Margaret A. Ormsby, British Columbia: A History (Toronto, 1958). Two fine general histories of architecture are Thomas Vaughan and Virginia Guest Ferriday, eds., Space, Style and Structure: Building in Northwest America (2 vols., Portland, 1974); and Kirker, California's Architectural Frontier. Lambert Florin, Historic Western Churches (Seattle, 1969), offers a selection of early churches in a popular vein.

The Russians are discussed in the general histories. Their churches are featured in Fern A. Wallace, The Flame of the Candle: A Pictorial History of Russian Orthodox Churches in Alaska (Chilliwack, BC, 1974). For Kenai, see Sister Victoria, "The Russian Experience," Orthodox Alaska (V:3-4, c. 1975), 15-33. Martin Florian tells The Story of St. Mary's Mission (Helena, 1965). See also Harold Allen, Father Ravalli's Missions (Chicago, 1972). Father Pandosy's mission is described in Primrose Upton, The History of Okanagan Mission (Kelowna, 1958), and in F.M. Buckland, Ogopogo's Vigil: A History of Kelowna and the Okanagan (1948; Kelowna, 1966). For the Oblate missions, see Kay Cronin, Cross in the Wilderness (Vancouver, 1960).

The best account of the Mormons' journey to Utah is Wallace Stegner, The Gathering of Zion: The Story of the Mormon Trail (New York, 1964). For the Mormon houses of worship, see Paul Goeldner, Utah Catalog: Historic American Buildings Survey (Salt Lake City, 1969); and Andrew and Blank, "The Four Mormon Temples."

Frank A. Peake, The Anglican Church in British Columbia (Vancouver, 1959), offers a good survey of the church's activities there. For the history of Barkerville, see Bruce Ramsey, Barkerville (Vancouver, 1961); and F.W. Ludditt, Barkerville Days (Vancouver, 1969). The history of the O'Keefe Ranch is summarized in the report prepared by Edward Mills and B.A. Humphreys for NHPSB.

List of Churches

Picture Credits

All of the photographs in this book were taken by John de Visser, with the exception of the following photos. Photos by Harold Kalman appear on pages: 13; 99; 108; 135 (bottom). Library of Congress photos appear on pages: 62; 63; 95 (bottom); 130 (bottom); 138 (bottom); 139; 168-169; 178; 180. Public Archives of Canada photos appear on pages: 88-89; 173 (bottom); 182 (bottom).

Also, photos on pages: 16, drawing by Champlain from *Voyages* (1613); 17, the Ursuline Convent, Quebec; 26 (left), *Inventaire des biens culturels*, Quebec; 98 (bottom), the Albany Institute; 135 (top, left) James Gibbs' *Book of Architecture* (1728); 136 (bottom), Indiana Division, Indiana State Library; 142 (top, left), Christ Church Cathedral (design by Frank Wills); 152-153 (top), Arizona Historical Society Library; 164, Missouri Historical Society; 165 (left) Perry County Lutheran Historical Society; 176, John L. Frisbee III for the Alaska Historical Commission; 179, Oregon Historical Society; 182 (top) State Historical Society of Colorado. Several line drawings were based on illustrations in other books. These are: p. 9, from Hugh Morrison, *Early American Architecture*; p. 32, from Ramsay Traquair, *The Old Architecture of Quebec*; p. 44, from G. Kubler, *The Religious Architecture of New Mexico*; p. 46, Rexford Newcomb, *The Old Mission Churches and Historic Houses of California*; p. 92, M.P. Corse, "The Old Ship Meeting-House in Hingham, Mass.", *Old Time New England*, xxi, 1, July, 1930; and p. 129, W.C. Kidney, *Historic Buildings of Ohio*.